WALKING THE CENTRAL SCOTTISH WAY

WALKING THE
Central Scottish Way

Erl B. Wilkie

MAINSTREAM
PUBLISHING
EDINBURGH AND LONDON

First published in Great Britain in 1996 by
MAINSTREAM PUBLISHING COMPANY (EDINBURGH) LTD
7 Albany Street
Edinburgh EH1 3UG

ISBN 1 85158 747 0

A catalogue record for this book is available from the British Library

Typeset in Stempel Garamond by Bibliocraft, Dundee
Printed and bound in Great Britain by Cromwell Press, Melksham

In memory of my late father, Robert, who is sadly missed by all the family

Two Ways

There was always two ways
back from school:
follow the pavements down
through lamposts
past the traffic wheeling down Brooms Road
then home-easy –
or slip through the Electric Yard
over the ancient wall
through forests and nettles swollen headed
and greasy grass belt high,
trace a path
past accents of birds
and rhythms before combustion.
There are always two ways,
one fast,
one best.

Hugh McMillan

CONTENTS

ACKNOWLEDGEMENTS

I am indebted to the following for their help in the preparation of this book: the Planning Departments, Library and Museum Departments and publications of the District and Regional Councils of Bearsden and Milngavie, Cumbernauld and Kilsyth, Falkirk, Glasgow, Strathkelvin, West Lothian, Midlothian, East Lothian, Edinburgh, Falkirk, Strathclyde, Lothian, Central and Borders.

A special thanks to the staff at the Edinburgh Room of the Central Library, Edinburgh; the Local History Department of West Lothian Libraries in Bathgate; the History and Topography Department; and the Glasgow Room of the Mitchell Library, Glasgow.

Also thanks to the British Waterways Board, the Forestry Commission, Wester Hailes Representative Council, the Union Canal Society, Linlithgow, and Lothian Regional Council Transportation Department.

A particular thanks to Keith Robson, Mike Baker and Susan Gray of Borders Regional Council Countryside Ranger Service. Thanks also to the many individuals I met along the route who gave me so much local information, and a special thanks to my friends Allan Mclean and Bruce Cuthbertson for their company along the way – especially to Allan for his many fine photographs!

To my wife, Anne, and daughter, Kirsten, I owe a special thanks for their continued support and understanding.

INTRODUCTION

The West Highland Way was the first of four long-distance walkways to be constructed in Scotland. Opened in 1980, it covers a distance of 95 miles, beginning at Fort William and ending in Milngavie, eight miles to the north-west of Glasgow. The others are the Southern Upland Way, the northern end of the Pennine Way and the Speyside Way.

This book highlights a fifth long-distance walkway which I have called the Central Scottish Way. This route runs between Milngavie and the Borders town of Jedburgh and continues to Byrness in Northumberland which is part of the Pennine Way. The route also uses the Southern Upland Way between Lauder and Melrose and so links together the West Highland Way, the Southern Upland Way and the Pennine Way.

It should be noted that the Central Scottish Way is not a formal walkway, therefore there may be localised closures along this route for the purposes of maintenance or other reasons.

Beginning at Milngavie, at the point where the West Highland Way ends, the Central Scottish Way uses, for the most part, a series of already formal public footpaths to reach its final destination in Byrness in Northumberland.

The Allander and Kelvin Walkway and the towpath of the Forth and Clyde Canal takes the route through Glasgow and

The Central Scottish Way

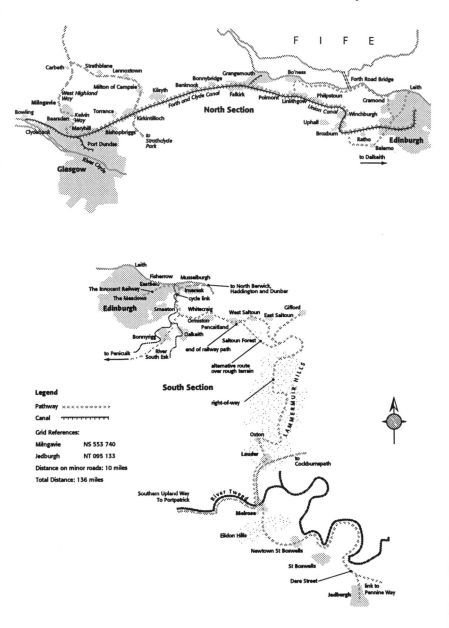

on to Falkirk. From there, the Union Canal leads to the heart of Edinburgh where the route continues across the city using the Meadows and the Innocent Railway Path. It then travels on into East Lothian along the River Esk Walkway and the Pencaitland Railway Walk.

A right-of-way over the Lammermuir Hills and a disused railway track bed takes it on to Lauder in the Borders. Here it connects with the Southern Upland Way, continues over the Eildon Hills and joins the walkway along the banks of the beautiful River Tweed at Newtown St Boswells where it continues to Maxton.

After this it joins Dere Street, the Roman road which once linked the River Tees with the Roman Fort at Musselburgh, for the last lap of the journey which travels high over the Cheviots to join the Pennine Way, the first official national trail in Britain opened in 1965, where it forges its way into England.

In turn, the Pennine Way links with Wainwright's Coast-to-Coast Walk which runs between the Lake District and the Yorkshire Coast before joining the Cleveland Way. This opens up a network of almost 1,000 miles of long-distance walkway.

As well as linking together these long-distance walkways, the Central Scottish Way can be used for a varied series of short walks, allowing access to the countryside – from lowland to highland and coastal to inland. Although the route goes straight through Edinburgh and Glasgow, it emerges on to the city streets for less than a quarter of a mile in Edinburgh and not at all in Glasgow. Three routes in and around Edinburgh have been included to provide the traveller with scenic short-distance walks, and those wishing to explore Glasgow further can consult my book, *Glasgow's Pathways*.

The Central Scottish Way also links together many of the most important and historical towns in Scotland.

As well as travelling through areas well frequented by tourists, the route also highlights those places which are, perhaps, less well known – for example it travels along the

Forth, Clyde and Union Canals, where much of Central Scotland's industrial heritage can be found, and passes many important historical sites, such as Antonine's Wall, as well as areas of special interest, such as the Bathgate Hills.

Taken either as a whole or in small, manageable parts, this walkway offers the walker a varied and interesting journey though the history of Scotland.

Most of the routes I have outlined are on public land or rights-of-way, except in the Borders where large stretches travel through private land. Although these routes are, for the most part, identified by waymarkers, access through much of this land is by permission of the landowners. This facility has been negotiated by the Borders Regional Council and it is, therefore, important to be especially vigilant within these areas.

A special plea comes from the farmers of the Border country. During the lambing season, please do not walk on Dere Street as it climbs over the Cheviots as this causes considerable distress to the sheep.

I would also like to point out that there is a law of trespass in Scotland, and although one cannot be prosecuted for crossing private land, one can be asked to leave or even be sued for damage through a civil court action.

I would, therefore, offer the following guidelines:

- If you come across a sign prohibiting access to a stretch of land, respect this and find an alternative route.
- If you are about to enter private land knowingly, try, if feasible, to gain the owner's permission before doing so.
- If, when you are walking within a route, you are challenged, unless you are completely sure the land you are walking on is public or is a right-of-way, then leave the private land by the shortest available route.
- When you are on any land, whether private or public, do not cause a nuisance in any way. Do not cause

16

damage to crops, property or fences. Close all gates and do not frighten farm animals. In other words, follow the country code.

- Keep dogs under control at all times.

If these commonsense rules are applied then no one can have any justifiable grievance against you.

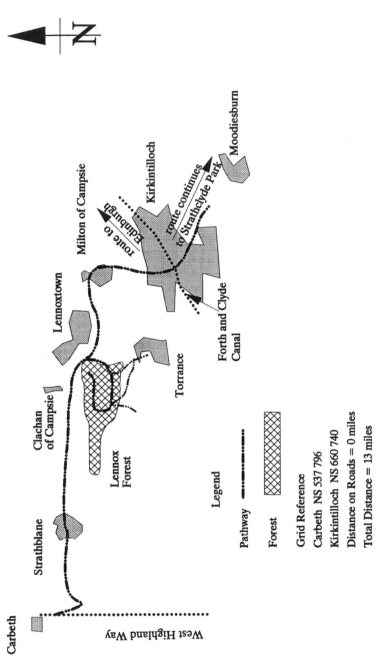

Legend

Pathway ▪▪▪▪▪▪▪

Forest ▨▨▨

Grid Reference
Carbeth NS 537 796
Kirkintilloch NS 660 740
Distance on Roads = 0 miles
Total Distance = 13 miles

West Highland Way

Carbeth

Strathblane

Clachan of Campsie

Lennoxtown

Milton of Campsie

Kirkintilloch

Moodiesburn

Lennox Forest

Torrance

Forth and Clyde Canal

route to Edinburgh

route continues to Strathclyde Park

N

CHAPTER ONE

West Highland Way to the Forth and Clyde Canal at Kirkintilloch

Starting at Carbeth the route takes the traveller eastward without having to go through Glasgow. Heading south, leave the West Highland Way just 100m after it crosses the B821, taking a footpath which forks to the left and goes through a gate. The path, though wide and clearly defined, rises through thick forest for about half a mile until it comes to a T-junction. At this point, turn left (turning right will take you to Mugdock Country Park) and follow this path for almost two miles to Strathblane as it winds down through the upper part of the village via Old Mugdock Road, and Dumbrock Road, until you reach the junction of the A81 (Glasgow, Aberfoyle Road) and the A891 (Strathblane to Lennoxtown Road). Strathblane means the wide valley of the River Blane.

Travel along the right-hand side of the A891 for some 50m, until you reach the point where the path recommences. Walk down this path for 100m to where it meets the disused Gartness to Kirkintilloch Railway which runs parallel to the road. This recently completed stretch goes from Strathblane all the way to Kirkintilloch, affording the traveller many comfortable miles. About a mile further on is the border with Strathkelvin District.

After about two-and-a-half miles the way crosses the first of many accesses into the Campsie hills – a farm road which

19

Clachan of Campsie old churchyard (with mausoleum of Lennox family)

leads to Clachan of Campsie. The ninth-century saint, Saint Machan, who was said to be one of the first native-born evangelists, built a place of worship here. In 1175 the first parish church was built on the site of his grave. After the Reformation another church was built in its place. Finally, when the High Church was built in the nineteenth century, the old church was allowed to fall into disrepair and only a gable is left standing. In the graveyard there is the old mausoleum of the Lennox family which dates back many centuries. Other interesting people also buried there include John Bell, the

Court Physician to the Russian Czar Peter the Great, and William Boick, covenanter and martyr.

Travel on a little further to Lennox Castle, which was the seat of the Lennox family until 1927 when it was sold. Glasgow Corporation developed it as a mental hospital in 1937 and it is still in use today. This house was built in 1841 on the same site as the previous house known as Woodhead which dated from the fifteenth century. The family resided in France during the two-year reconstruction period.

The way goes on via Lennoxtown, previously known as Newton of Campsie. This village was once noted for calico printing and hand-loom weaving, but these industries have completely vanished. The village is now mainly a residential area for Kirkintilloch and Glasgow. Lennoxtown is another place where the traveller can gain access to the Campsie Hills.

At the point where the way reaches the village, the traveller will come to a second bridge over the path (the first being at Lennox Castle). By way of a detour, the traveller could climb

New stretch of walkway at Lennox Castle

21

to the road above and turn right, following the road as it winds to the top of the hill to reach Lennox Forest. Here there are many walks through the woods.

At Muirhead Farm there is a signpost pointing out a right-of-way which heads down the valley to Torrance. Ignore this and continue to follow the forestry road, keeping the radar

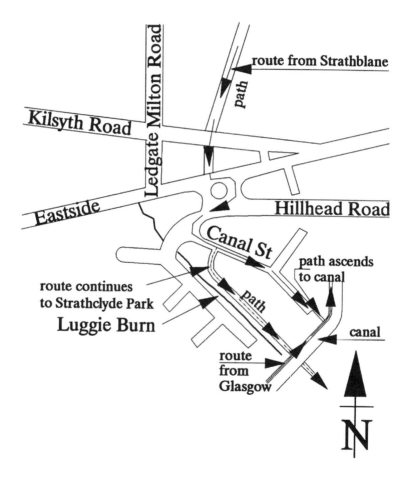

station on the left. Here, on a clear day, one can see over the entire city of Glasgow.

Travel on till you come to a single-bar gate across the road and, passing this, carry straight on for another 200m. Then take the road to the left and follow it as it winds downhill past a disused quarry on the right. This road is known as Mealy Brae.

After about two miles or so it comes out on to the A81, at the junction with the Mugdock road, which in turn takes the traveller back to Mugdock Country Park.

If, however, the traveller wishes to continue along the Central Scottish Way, then carry on past the second bridge until you reach Milton of Campsie. This is another village with much the same history as Lennoxtown, although it is said that in the eighteenth century it was a great centre for whisky smuggling. From Milton it is barely a mile along a pleasant wooded path to reach Kirkintilloch where the footpath joins the Kilsyth Road.

The traveller should then take the path adjacent to Ledgate, continuing across Eastside and going into Canal Street. At the top of Canal Street there is a ramp up to the Forth and Clyde Canal where the route continues eastward.

The remainder of this route to Strathclyde Park and also the link with the Clyde Walkway is described in my book, *Glasgow's Pathways*.

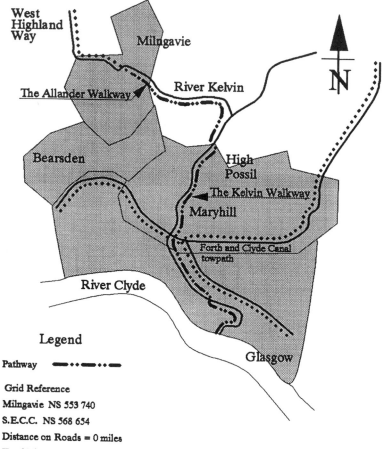

West
Highland
Way

Milngavie

The Allander Walkway

River Kelvin

N

Bearsden

High
Possil

The Kelvin Walkway

Maryhill

Forth and Clyde Canal
towpath

River Clyde

Glasgow

Legend

Pathway

Grid Reference
Milngavie NS 553 740
S.E.C.C. NS 568 654
Distance on Roads = 0 miles
Total Distance = 13 miles

CHAPTER TWO

The Allander and Kelvin Walkway

The West Highland Way starts or finishes at Douglas Street in the heart of Milngavie. It is marked by an obelisk which was erected on 20 November 1992. This is also the point where the Central Scottish Way begins, although as yet no sign for it exists. Therefore, the traveller will have to make do with my directions. But first the history!

The tiny hamlet of Milngavie as it existed in the middle of the eighteenth century had probably remained unchanged for many hundreds of years but within a space of about 25 years it underwent a dramatic upheaval due to the cotton industry. By the last quarter of the century there were six small bleachfields and two printworks in the vicinity of the Allander Burn.

There is much speculation about the name Milngavie and it was certainly shown on some old maps as being spelt Millguy. I feel, however, this is more likely to have been the cartographer's error as the Gaelic word for mill is *muileann*, which could account for the first half of the name. The second part could be derived from *gavilhe* which means wind or windy.

Due to the influx of Glaswegians wishing to reside in a more rural atmosphere, the village and surrounding district became much larger by the middle of the nineteenth century, and was made a police burgh in 1862. With the building of the

The West Highland Way as it goes through Milngavie

railway the village continued to grow into the small town we know today.

In the early part of the twentieth century Glasgow's tramcars were extended to Milngavie to accommodate the vastly increased numbers of commuters wishing to travel to the city. However, Milngavie began to be seen by Glasgow's working class as a stepping-out point for areas such as Mugdock and Loch Lomond and by the 1930s there were six times as many trams to Milngavie on a Sunday as there were during weekdays.

Straddling the Glasgow to Milngavie Railway, roughly where the Allander Sports Centre is situated today, was the test track of the *Bennie Railplane*. This prototype bullet train was tested here during the 1930s but the Second World War

Idyllic view of the River Kelvin at Killermont

27

halted further development. The track was finally demolished in the late 1950s.

Turn right along the pedestrianised Douglas Street and then take a left into Main Street. Follow this street to its end, passing the Black Bull Hotel, to find an underpass. Take this brightly coloured underpass with its murals depicting scenes of the countryside and coast. Within a few metres you will reach the other side where there is a footbridge which crosses the Allander Burn and goes into Lennox Park. Here you will find the first direction pole for the Allander Walkway with its distinctive Heron logo. This walkway is well signposted and makes it easy to identify the route all the way into Glasgow.

The path follows the Allander Burn past Balmore Road to where the burn enters the River Kelvin. From here the signing of the route changes to portray a flying duck as the route becomes the Kelvin Walkway. It then follows the banks of the River Kelvin for about half a mile to another part of Balmore Road at the Brasher Bridge, at which point it joins the opposite bank of the river.

This is where the Antonine Wall once crossed the River Kelvin and here, just as the path begins on the other side of Balmore Road, are the remains of Balmuildy Fort which is one of only two stone-built forts along the wall. This fort was excavated at the turn of the century and many important artefacts were discovered there, but it was subsequently filled in and today there is very little of it left exposed.

After almost a mile the path goes through a picturesque wooded area which bounds the riverside and which is home to many varieties of birds, including the kingfisher. Here, beyond the opposite bank, one catches sight of Killermont Estate which is now home to Glasgow's most exclusive golf club.

The route then passes the Glasgow Headquarters for Riding for the Disabled, where the staff and a dedicated band of volunteers do a wonderful job. After passing the stables, the way joins Caldercuilt Road and then goes into Maryhill Park. The traveller will notice that the route has deviated from the riverbank. This is necessary because there is no way through

28

Statue of Bud Neil's Lobey Dosser in Woodlands Road

the Garscube Estate, which now belongs to the University of Glasgow. Alas, some very beautiful scenery is missed due to this deviation.

The river runs through the estate for almost a mile and, for reasons best known to themselves, the university wishes this land to remain private. This is unfortunate for the traveller because, despite the fact that the house has been demolished, the estate is very much as it was in the nineteenth century, including its Home Farm.

Busy city bridges over the tranquil Kelvin Walkway

Leave Maryhill Park by the gate which leads on to Maryhill Road – the road is easily crossed at the traffic lights – and continue into Dalsholm Road. After only 200m or so, the route again continues along the banks of the River Kelvin.

The walkway also follows the line of the old Caledonian Railway which served local industry in the nineteenth and twentieth centuries until its decline just after the First World War. Half a mile further on the route passes under the aqueduct which carries the Forth and Clyde Canal above the Kelvin. At this point the traveller should take a path on the left to transfer to the canal towpath.

From here, however, the traveller may wish to explore the delights of Scotland's largest city and so I shall describe this walkway to where it ends in the heart of Glasgow.

The walkway continues east, first crossing Kelvindale Road and then passing, on the left, some blocks of high flats which were built on the site of Maryhill Barracks. This was the home, until 1959, of Glasgow's own regiment, the Highland Light Infantry.

Travel on another quarter of a mile to a footbridge which crosses the river. This is one of the entrances to the Botanic Gardens – one of Glasgow's beautiful Victorian parks with such attractions as the Kibble Palace which houses many species of tropical plants.

At this footbridge, there are also some swings – the scene of a very amusing and perhaps typically Glaswegian incident which was witnessed by me. While researching the chapter on the Kelvin Walkway I was walking past these swings one day. It was a Saturday and there were quite a few kids around. Suddenly, a pit bull terrier appeared, running towards the swings. Not surprisingly the kids scattered in all directions, leaving the swings free. The dog then took hold of one of the swings and, with its teeth firmly implanted in the seat, began to swing vigorously back and forward. Its grip only loosened when the animal bit clean through the rubber seat of the swing, at which point it took a fresh grip and started again. From across the footbridge over the Kelvin two drunks ambled up to the scene and addressed me, saying, 'Oh, he's aright, pal. He'll no do anything to the kids, he just likes a wee swing ye know! Would ye like a wee drink, pal?'

I was down in the same area about a fortnight later and I noticed that two of the three swings had by this time no seats at all and a third was only half its normal breadth. This dog certainly did like a wee swing!

Kelvin Bridge flats (formally the annex to the Central Hotel)

As the route continues, it passes under the first of the many beautiful, red-sandstone Victorian bridges which span the river along this stretch of the walkway. These bridges carry the busy city streets high above, for we are now almost in the heart of Glasgow. A quarter of a mile further on the walkway itself crosses the river and from here the remnants of an old mill lade can still be seen. This is North Woodside Flint Mill which was in operation until the beginning of this century.

This last mile-long stretch of the Kelvin, until the point where it joins the Clyde, holds great historical significance for Glasgow as it was the site of the town's sixteenth-century flour mills. In 1568 the Earl of Moray, Regent of Scotland, gave his permission for the first of these flour mills to be built. This favour was bestowed on the burghers of Glasgow for their great service to him at the battle of Langside where his forces defeated Mary Queen of Scots's army, led by the fifth Earl of Argyll. A succession of mills were built on these sites, the last of which was still operating as late as the nineteenth century.

After passing under Kelvin Bridge, which takes Great Western Road over the river, the walkway reaches Kelvingrove Park. At the other side of the park is Kelvingrove Museum and Art Gallery which was built to coincide with Glasgow's second Great International Exhibition in 1901. It houses one of the finest collections of paintings, including works by Botticelli, Giorgione, Rembrandt, Millet, Monet, Van Gogh, Derain, Picasso and Dali.

Situated on Gilmour Hill, overlooking the park, is Glasgow University. It moved to this location in 1870, leaving its original site in the High Street where it had been located since 1460, although the university had been in existence in the Chapter House and Lower Church of the Cathedral since 1451. It is Scotland's second oldest university, after St Andrews. The university houses the Hunterian Museum, where many of the relics found at various sections of the Antonine Wall can be seen.

On leaving Kelvingrove Park, cross Dumbarton Road into Bunhouse Road which is the home of the Kelvin Hall. The

Glasgow University

original building was destroyed by fire in July 1925 and the present building was opened by King George V exactly two years later. Its primary function, until it was superseded by the Scottish Exhibition and Conference Centre in 1986, was as an exhibition centre. In 1986 renovations began to change the building to suit its present function as a Museum of Transport.

Turn right into Old Dumbarton Road and then left into Yorkhill Park, at the end of which is Sandyford Street. Turn right here and at the bottom of this street there is a footbridge over the Clydeside Expressway. Although the footbridge marks the end of the Kelvin Walkway, it is just the beginning of the Clyde Walkway, the Glasgow to Loch Lomond Cycleway and the Glasgow to Irvine Cycleway.

From here it is but a short walk to Glasgow city centre.

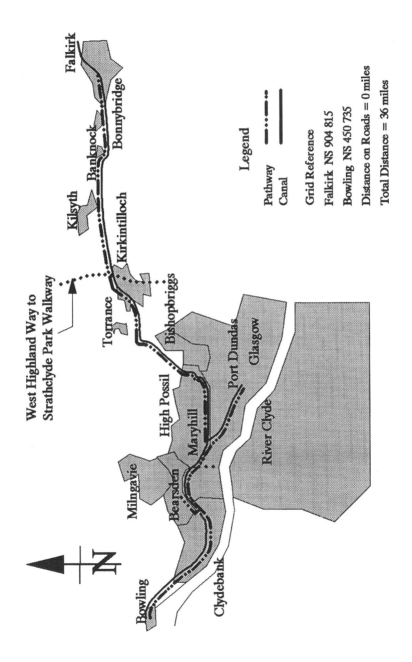

West Highland Way to
Strathclyde Park Walkway

N

Falkirk
Bonnybridge
Banknock
Kilsyth
Kirkintilloch
Torrance
Bishopbriggs
Port Dundas
Glasgow
High Possil
Maryhill
River Clyde
Milngavie
Bearsden
Clydebank
Bowling

Legend

Pathway
Canal

Grid Reference
Falkirk NS 904 815
Bowling NS 450 735
Distance on Roads = 0 miles
Total Distance = 36 miles

CHAPTER THREE

The Forth and Clyde Canal Towpath

To deal with the canal in isolation is impossible, for the area through which it passes is steeped in so much of Scotland's history that it would be remiss of me not to bring some of it to the walker's attention. The canal follows the same route as the Antonine Wall, marking the shortest distance between the east and west coasts of Scotland.

Before the Forth and Clyde Canal was built, ships wishing to get from the west coast to the east would have had to sail round the top of Scotland – a distance in excess of 300 miles and a very arduous and dangerous journey, especially in rough weather. The proposed line of the canal, on the other hand, was only 35 miles long.

The engineer in charge of the design and construction was John Smeaton, who some years before had designed and built the Eddystone lighthouse. Digging began at Grangemouth on the River Forth in 1768 and it took 22 years to complete, finishing at Bowling on the River Clyde in 1790, where the company chairman poured a hog's head of Forth water into the Clyde.

The major part of the canal, from Grangemouth to Stockingfield where the main canal joins the Glasgow branch, was completed by 1775, but the Forth and Clyde Canal Company ran out of money and work stopped for 10

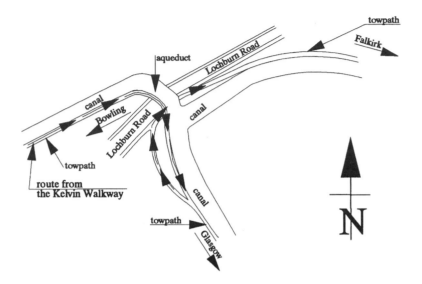

years. During this time the Glasgow branch was extended as far as Hamilton by an Act of Parliament. In 1791 Port Dundas was constructed together with the junction with the Monkland Canal.

As its name suggests, Port Dundas was built as a port. It took its name from the first governor of the Canal Company, Sir Thomas Dundas, and was built at One-Hundred-Acre Hill above the City of Glasgow. Wharves, basins, granaries and warehouses were constructed. It also had a customs house, a toll-collector's house, and a bridge-keeper's house. At this time a toll-collector, bridge-keeper, and lock-keeper's wage was six shillings and sixpence per week, plus their house.

The canal was used extensively by passenger boats as the quickest and most comfortable way to travel between Glasgow and Edinburgh. In 1848 the Edinburgh to Glasgow Railway had opened and the Canal Company stopped its passenger service. All passenger services stopped in 1876.

Pleasure steamers were introduced in 1893 and ran to the beginning of the Second World War.

Until recently the canal was bounded by factories manufacturing rubber products, oil by-products, a dye works, grain mills and a distillery. In its heyday this part of the canal would have been bustling. Sadly, much of this industry has now disappeared. However, since the factories have stopped depositing harmful waste into the canal, it now supports varieties of flora and fauna unknown for the last 150 years.

Leave the Kelvin Walkway, climb up on to the aqueduct and carry on along the towpath in an easterly direction. This aqueduct carries the Forth and Clyde Canal 75 feet above the river on a 400-foot-long, four-arched stone structure which was completed in 1790.

Travelling in this direction, the first interesting feature one comes to is the Maryhill Lock Flight. This is the highest part of the canal, the summit level being some 156 feet above sea level. Maryhill docks were constructed in 1790, at the same time as the flight of locks. This is known locally as the Botany, for it was one of the points of embarkation for people travelling to Botany Bay in Australia.

The Maryhill Lock Flight had been allowed to fall into a state of disrepair since the canal's closure in the 1960s, but recently they have been partially reconstructed as part of the Glasgow Canal Project.

The Glasgow Canal Project was started in 1988 and is jointly funded by the British Waterways Board, the former Strathclyde Regional Council and the Manpower Services Commission. Its aim is to reopen 12 miles of the canal to shipping with the reconstruction of three bridges with increased headroom and replacing the lock gates at Maryhill (much of this work is already finished). When the work is complete pleasure boats will once again be able to sail all the way from Kirkintilloch to the heart of Glasgow and west to Anniesland.

It will surprise you how many varieties of waterfowl you

Mort-safe and guardroom, Cadder Parish Church

encounter along the canal; there are coots, moorhens, ducks and swans, even before you arrive at Ruchill.

Carry on another quarter of a mile to Stockingfield to where the Glasgow branch joins the main canal.

To get on to the eastern towpath at Stockingfield junction head down the ramp on to Lochburn Road, turn right to go under the canal bridge and, staying on the same side of the road, walk up the ramp to the canal towpath on the other side of the canal.

After a mile or so, the canal passes under Balmore Road Bridge and enters the district of High Possil, passing close by to Possil Loch, a large area of marsh which is a Scottish Wildlife Trust Reserve where huge stocks of wildfowl winter and breed. If you carry on for almost two miles to reach Balmouldie Road, Bishopbriggs, you will find Bishopbriggs Sports Centre which contains various sporting amenities, including a large swimming-pool.

Another mile further on is Cadder Church. At the beginning of the nineteenth century the graveyard was the scene of bodysnatching. Bodies were stolen before they were buried, or dug up after burial; victims were even murdered to satisfy the doctors' demand. The most famous of these bodysnatchers, as they were known, were Burke and Hare. Because of its close proximity to the canal, Cadder Church was an ideal spot for bodysnatching – the canal being a fast and convenient way to transport corpses to both Edinburgh and Glasgow. Indeed, this happened so often that the people of Cadder had a watch house and iron mort-safes built to protect the coffins from attack. These can still be seen in the churchyard.

In 1820 a ship docked in Liverpool was found to contain a cargo of bodies which were thought to have come from Dublin.

Thomas Muir, the Scottish leader of the eighteenth-century campaign for parliamentary reform, was once an elder at Cadder Church. He lived in Bishopbriggs at Huntershill House, which his father had bought in 1782. Today this house has been turned into a museum devoted to his life and work.

Born in Glasgow in 1765, Muir studied divinity at Glasgow University and law at Edinburgh University. He was admitted to the Faculty of Advocates in 1787.

Whilst at the bar in Edinburgh he soon built up a good legal practice, often representing the poor – he was one of the very few of his profession who did. Many of his clients were strikers or people with grievances against the political system of the time.

He mixed with people who were no lovers of the Union and were greatly influenced by the French Revolution, believing that political reform was urgently required in Scotland.

In 1792 Muir set up the Edinburgh Friends of the People and the Associated Friends of the Constitution and of the People, in Glasgow. At the organisations' first National Convention in December 1792, the authorities, who were nervous of any form of agitation, arrested Muir and others, charging them with sedition. While he was on bail, pending his trial, he went to France. He was delayed there, failed to appear on the day fixed for his trial and was declared an outlaw in Britain. On his return to Scotland, Muir was found guilty of sedition and was sentenced to 14 years' deportation.

In 1794 he and other leaders of the Scottish reform movement were sent out to Botany Bay in Australia.

After 16 months in the penal colony Muir managed to escape on an American ship. He intended to join George Washington whom, he felt, would welcome him as a brother revolutionary. The ship took him to a small port on the north-west coast of America from where he sailed to Mexico. When the ship docked at Mexico, the captain, who suspected Muir of being a spy, handed him over to the authorities. He remained in Havana jail for four months before being transported to Spain.

When his release was negotiated by the French Government, he arrived in France to a hero's welcome. From Paris he continued to support radical movements, liaising between the French Government and British and Irish political exiles. In 1799 he died in Chantilly at the age of 33.

A memorial was erected in his honour in Edinburgh by the

The Stables, Glasgow Bridge

Friends Parliamentary Reform in England and Scotland and the inscription quotes words spoken by Muir at his trial: 'I have devoted myself to the cause of the people; it is a good cause; it shall finally triumph.'

Continue on from Cadder to the stables at Glasgow Road Bridge. From 1831 until 1848 a fleet of horse-drawn boats called 'swifts' sailed between Glasgow and Falkirk. As their name suggests, they had a reputation for speed. In order to maintain their high speed (around ten miles per hour), the horses towing the boats had to be changed regularly. The Georgian building now converted into The Stables restaurant and bar was the place where the horses were exchanged.

This building was restored in 1981, at the time when boats returned to the canal. A restaurant barge and some pleasure boats operate from here, but with Glasgow Bridge – the third of the new bridges – now finished, these boats can once again carry on to Kirkintilloch, about a mile further on.

In the twelfth century this area, and all the way to Cumbernauld, was in the hands of the Comyn family who had their castle at Kirkintilloch. The moat is still visible at Peel Park. William Comyn granted the town burgh status in 1211, although it dates back much further than that. Its name was originally Caerpentulach – 'the fort on the ridge' – the 'fort' being part of Antonine's Wall.

Kirkintilloch remained a small predominantly agricultural and weaving community until the advent of the canal. In 1773, while work had stopped further west on the canal, Kirkintilloch was operating as Scotland's first inland port with access to the River Forth and the east. In 1860 the first shipbuilding and repair yard was opened and ships were built in Kirkintilloch until the Second World War.

Sadly, the canal is still culverted under Townhead in Kirkintilloch, but just beyond this point a new bridge has been constructed, part of the Kirkintilloch Relief Road Project, which has sufficient headroom to let boats through. Perhaps another bridge will be built at Townhead.

The canal goes on by way of Twechar, a small mining and quarrying village, and passes close to Barr Hill and Croy Hill, each of which has a Roman fort. This area possesses good stretches of the Antonine Wall which can be seen within a short distance from the canal. To reach the forts, cross over the canal at the bridge in Twechar. Continue on the left side of this road for about 100m until you see a track going off to the left. Follow this track for a quarter of a mile up a long hill to reach a covered circular concrete reservoir. Then take the path to the left, go through a gate and walk on another 50m to Barr Hill Fort.

It's a worthwhile detour as there is a great deal to see: the layouts of the fort and bath-house are clearly defined and some of the stonework is still in place. Carry on to the top of the next hill, which is marked by a concrete cairn, to the site of an Iron Age fort which predates the Roman one. From here the ditch in front of the wall is clearly visible. There is also a very good view of the canal and the surrounding countryside below.

Follow the path, continuing in the direction you have come. After skirting a wood on the right, go down the hill to join a larger path which in turn meets up with the A802 at Croy. Turn left at Croy and head for Auchinstarry, where the walkway once again runs alongside the canal. Follow the canal as it passes under the B802 (the Kilsyth to Cumbernauld road) at Auchinstarry, where it is spanned by a non-opening bascule bridge.

Some 300m away in the direction of Kilsyth is a disused quarry which has been turned into a leisure area by the former Kilsyth and Cumbernauld District Council. The floor of the quarry is under water, and this small loch is framed by landscaped areas in the foreground with a 100ft-high whinstone face exposed behind. It is very pleasant to see a disused industrial site – previously a blot on the landscape – turned into such an attractive and interesting place.

The whinstone or dolerite which was quarried here was worked into kerbs and paving-stones, which were taken on barges along the canal to pave the streets of Glasgow.

Canal boats on the Forth and Clyde Canal

Travel on another mile and a half to Craigmalloch where the canal crosses the road to Dullatur. This is where the main source of water enters the canal, the inlet being right beside the road and running in a lade from Banton Loch, a mile to the north. Banton Loch, or Townhead Reservoir as it is also known, is in its present form man-made. It is a very picturesque loch with a pleasant walk around its banks. The locals use it extensively for fishing, but are always complaining that they never catch anything!

To reach the loch from the canal, first turn north and walk for about half a mile to reach the A803, Kilsyth to Falkirk road. Opposite the junction of the walkway and the A803 you will find an unsignposted track. Take this track for a quarter of a mile to reach the south-west side of the loch.

If you continue further north on this track, you will climb into the Kilsyth Hills, where there are many fine walks into the Campsie Fells, through the Carron Valley Forest and Loch Carron. Even if you are not in the mood for a long climb, it is interesting to walk on for a mile or so, just to see the spectacular view over practically the whole of the Forth and Clyde Valley.

Kilsyth also lies about half a mile away to the north and can be reached easily from either Craigmalloch or Auchinstarry. There are many explanations of the town's name: the most popular view is that *kil* means 'church' or 'chapel' and *sythe* is a reference to a mythical saint of that name. Others think that it changed its name in the sixteenth century from Moniebrugh which meant 'hilly place of streams'.

The true definition, however, is that there were two estates adjoining one another, the westerly Kelvesith (meaning 'Kelvin Sands') being changed to the present Kilsyth. The estate to the east was indeed Moniebrugh. In 1620 Sir William Livingston, the owner of Kilsyth Castle since the beginning of the century, acquired the Moniebrugh estate as well and the two were merged, with the whole area being known as Kilsyth.

The Battle of Kilsyth, which was part of the Civil War, was fought close to the town in 1645. Around the reservoir area are places named Slaughter Howe, Bullet Knowe and Drum Burn, testifying to the ferocity of the battle. Those soldiers and cavalry who fled the battlefield when defeat looked imminent were trapped in the nearby Dullatur Bog. Some 125 years later when the canal was being cut through the bog, a number of those unfortunate troopers were discovered exactly where they were submerged, including one apparently still seated on his horse.

Dullatur Bog was one of the most difficult obstacles encountered by John Smeaton while constructing the canal. The land was so wet and soft that nothing could be built on it without sinking and it had to be completely drained. Unfortunately for the local inhabitants this disturbed millions of tiny toads from their natural environment in the bog and caused them to invade the houses and lands of the people living

The Antonine Wall at Seabegs Wood

48

round about. So great was the problem that a complaint was sent to the canal authorities.

Stone banks were then constructed which kept sinking into the ground. It was estimated that they sank to a depth of 50ft below ground-level in some places before they were consolidated and could form the actual canal bank.

Head for Castlecary, some five miles to the east of Kilsyth. On route you will pass the small village of Kelvinhead, the source of the River Kelvin in Dullatur Bog just to the south, and then on under the A80 Glasgow to Stirling road. Here you will find Wyndford Lock (Lock 20), the first lock for 16 miles since leaving Maryhill in Glasgow.

Castlecary takes its name from the castle which was built in 1473 by the Livingston family and which is still standing today. Deriving from the old word *caer*, meaning 'fort', Castlecary means the castle of the fort – referring to the stones of a Roman fort from which the castle was built.

A couple of miles further on is Underwood Lockhouse. Formerly the home of the lock keeper, the building has been turned into a very fine bar and restaurant offering a welcome break from the canal-side journey.

From here it is not long before you approach an aqueduct which goes beneath the canal to Seabegs Wood. At this point the Antonine Wall, which runs adjacent to the canal, is very clearly defined. This is the site of a fortlet excavated in 1977, which is well worth a look.

The route passes High Bonnybridge, a small mining and foundry town, from where another Roman fort can be reached: Rough Castle is a 20-minute walk from the canal, and is clearly signposted. Access is along a farm road, then via a rough track to a carpark. Along this track lies Bonnybridge House, and between it and Rough Castle is the best preserved section of the Antonine Wall: the rampart and ditch, the remains of two signalling platforms, and even traces of the military way can be seen.

Although one of the smallest forts along the length of the wall, Rough Castle offers the sightseer a very good picture of the fort and its defences. An unusual feature are the pits which were dug in the north-west corner of the site. Each pit contained a sharpened stake concealed below ground-level, and was designed to prevent any attack on the vulnerable gateway through the wall. Finds from the fort can be seen in the Royal Museum of Scotland in Edinburgh.

Back to the canal as it crosses the B816 at High Bonnybridge, one should look out for a colourful mural on the exterior walls of the foundry by the bridge over the canal.

Three miles further on takes the towpath to Falkirk via Camelon. Falkirk (or Fawe Kirk, meaning 'speckled church') has been a burgh since 1600. The town had been in existence for many centuries before that date, however, and has had more than its fair share of events that have shaped Scotland's history. As well as being the site of a Roman fort, the town also gave its name to two famous battles, although the actual geographical locations of these could hardly be said to be in Falkirk itself.

The first battle was in 1298 when William Wallace's forces fought the biggest English army to be assembled thus far in Scotland – 25,000 infantry and almost 6,000 cavalry – under Edward I, the so-called 'Hammer of the Scots'. Wallace's forces sustained dreadful losses, and the graves of many of the fallen Scots can still be seen in the old churchyard in Falkirk.

The outcome of the second Battle of Falkirk, in January 1746, could not be more different. Bonnie Prince Charlie's Jacobite forces defeated the Government troops led by General Hawley on a day of gale force winds and driving rain. Their victory was short-lived, however, as a mere three months later, on 16 April 1746, the Jacobites were resoundingly beaten at Culloden by an army commanded by the Duke of Cumberland who had been sent north to replace the disgraced Hawley. Bonnie Prince Charlie made good his escape and lived as a fugitive for a year, eventually being taken to safety in France.

Falkirk became famous for the Tryst, which was the national meeting place for the sale of farm animals and the gathering place for drovers and dealers from all parts, from the Western Isles and Ross-shire in the north to Yorkshire in the south. The fair, first held on Redding Moor just south of Falkirk, was then moved to Rough Castle and later, in 1785, was transferred to its final location in Stenhousemuir, where it remained till 1900. There were no auctioneers and cattle were sold only after a bargain was struck between the dealer and the drover and a 'dram' was drunk. The Tryst took place on the second Tuesday of August, September and October. Today it is limited to a single weekend, which it shares with the fair.

In the eighteenth and nineteenth centuries Falkirk was the centre of the iron industry in Scotland, due to the plentiful supply of iron ore being mined in the district, and many companies used the canal to transport their products. Today Falkirk is a fine town, mixing the modern with the traditional. Most of the industry in the area is confined to Grangemouth and other surrounding areas.

Nowadays, the Forth and Clyde Canal ends its 35-mile journey in Falkirk, the last few miles to the River Forth being culverted. Before it finishes it descends through a picturesque series of locks, starting at Lock 16. Opposite these locks is the Union Inn, from where the Forth and Clyde Canal was linked to the Union Canal at Greenbank. If the traveller wishes to continue the journey east to Edinburgh along the banks of the Union Canal, then there are over 30 interesting miles to go.

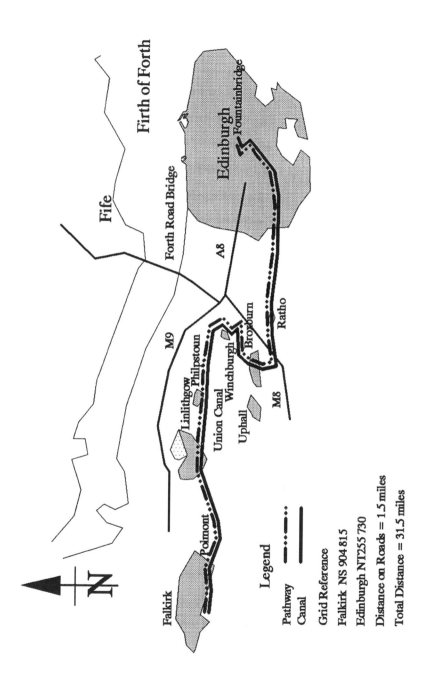

Firth of Forth

Fife

Forth Road Bridge

Edinburgh

Fountainbridge

A8

M9

Falkirk

Polmont

Linlithgow

Philpstoun

Union Canal

Winchburgh

Uphall

Broxburn

Ratho

M8

N

Legend

Pathway

Canal

Grid Reference

Falkirk NS 904 815

Edinburgh NT255 730

Distance on Roads = 1.5 miles

Total Distance = 31.5 miles

CHAPTER FOUR

The Union Canal

In relation to other British Canals, the Union Canal was a latecomer. Work was started on 3 March 1818 and it finally opened in January 1822. The canal was first envisaged as a cheap method of transporting coal to Edinburgh. The success of this idea had been proved by the Forth and Clyde Canal, which since 1790 had been used extensively as a cheap means of transporting large loads of coal and other raw materials to Glasgow. At the end of the eighteenth century, coal bound for Edinburgh had risen sharply in price, due to a very restricted market and the laborious nature of overland transportation. A direct link between Glasgow and Edinburgh would facilitate bulk transportation of coal and would also open up the Lanarkshire collieries to the city of Edinburgh.

Preliminary discussions started as early as 1791. In 1793, a committee was appointed to employ engineers to prepare a report on the best route of the proposed canal.

In the course of the next five years a total of five different routes were suggested, by which time the beginning of the Napoleonic War meant the project was shelved for another 15 years.

Once the canal was finally opened in 1822 it enjoyed brief but considerable popularity, with as many as 200,000 people using it in 1836. However, the opening of the Glasgow to

The Union Inn

Edinburgh Railway in 1842 eventually led to a decline in the use of the canal which was eventually closed to navigation in 1965.

Once the traveller has left the Forth and Clyde Canal, the way is still open to continue the journey to Edinburgh along the towpath of the Union Canal.

The junction of the two canals, known as Port Downie, was created by a series of 11 locks which raised the canal 110ft in less than half a mile. These locks were closed in 1933 and were subsequently filled in. Although it was a great feat of civil engineering, it was a very slow and laborious process to get the barges up and down. It became normal for passengers to alight from the barge at the bottom of the hill at the Union

Inn and, after a brief coach journey, join another barge at the top of the hill for the second leg of the journey to Edinburgh.

Today the Union Inn still provides refreshment for the traveller.

After leaving the inn turn right and immediately right again on to Greenbank Road. The road winds its way uphill to meet the Union Canal a quarter of a mile further on.

Once on the towpath it is approximately one mile to the Canal Tunnel. This tunnel, measuring 18ft wide by 19ft high, had to be constructed, at great cost, through Prospect Hill because William Forbes, the owner of the adjacent Callendar Estate, would not countenance the canal passing within sight of Callendar House.

The tunnel travels for almost a third of a mile through solid rock. On entering, the traveller will notice a constant sound of running water and an intense darkness. However, a guard rail runs the entire length.

The canal then winds its way through another three miles of countryside to Polmont, passing the Glen Bridge which displays a happy face on its eastern keystone and an unhappy face on the western one and is known as 'the Laughin and Greetin Bridge'. It is the largest of the single-arch bridges over the canal.

Polmont is said to be located on the site of a Roman fort. There is no trace left of this ancient fortification and indeed there is nothing much known about Polmont until the advent of the Edinburgh to Glasgow Railway.

Travel on a further two miles to reach Muiravonside Old Parish Church. Here there is a picnic area where you can enjoy the peace and beauty of the surrounding countryside.

A little further on the canal is once again broken by a culvert which carries the Linlithgow to Maddiston road. On this road, about 25m on the left going towards Maddiston, is a sign which states 'Public footpath to Muiravonside Country Park, 1km'.

A short distance further on the canal is broken once again by a culvert under the B825, after which it meanders through some beautiful tree-lined, idyllically quiet countryside for

Scene at Muiravonside Country Park

another mile or so until it crosses 85ft above the Avon Valley on the largest of the canal's three aqueducts.

The Avon Aqueduct, spanning the valley on 12 arches, is some 900ft in length and is the longest and tallest Scottish aqueduct. It offers some very fine views over the Avon Valley. This is the first of the three large multi-span structures which were built as part of the original canal. The other two carry the canal across the Almond Valley and the Water of Leith at Slateford.

Leave the aqueduct and pass Woodcockdale Stables in which the horses used for pulling the barges along the canal were kept. From here it is only a short distance to Linlithgow.

The route of the canal at Linlithgow travels along the higher land to the south of the town centre, but even so it had to be built on an embankment. In the early 1980s the embankment to the west of the town collapsed over a distance of some 200m and this stretch of the canal had to be dammed and de-watered. The canal remained like this for some years until, as part of the West Lothian Project, British Waterways and the local authorities rebuilt the embankment. A new bridge was also constructed over Preston Road as part of this project which replaced the culvert installed in the 1960s. (Preston Road is the way to Beecraigs Country Park. If travelling in an easterly direction turn right on to Preston Road and continue for just over a mile to the entrance to the park.)

Linlithgow means 'the double lake in the hollow', and in this fertile part of the country there would doubtless have existed a settlement from the very earliest times. Indeed, there are traces of a Roman settlement in this vicinity: Roman hill-forts have been discovered close to the town and in the eighteenth century a farmer in the area ploughed up an urn containing 300 Roman coins.

In 1868 a Legionary Tablet was found at Bridgeness at the eastern end of Bo'ness on the site of the Antonine Wall and is marked by a plaque in Harbour Road, Bo'ness. The tablet is the largest to have been discovered intact and can be seen in the Royal Scottish Museum of Antiquities in Edinburgh.

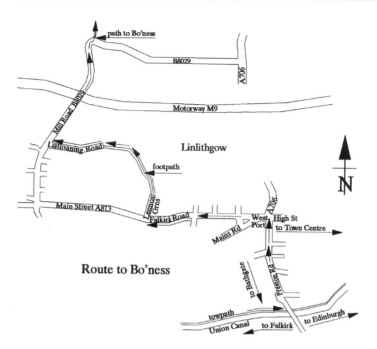

Route to Bo'ness

Illustrated by a victorious Roman soldier riding over the top of naked dead and wounded Britons while the Second Legion offers up a sacrifice to the gods, it is inscribed: 'To the Emperor Caesar Titus Aelius Hadrianus Antoninus Austus Pius, father of his country. Legion II the Augustan throughout four thousand paces made' (they built four thousand paces – 7km – of wall).

The area around Linlithgow is said to have been defended by King Arthur in a succession of battles against Picts and Scots from the north and Angles from the south. Indeed, legend would have it that Arthur was eventually slain at the battle of Camlan in 537 – Camlan possibly being Camelon near Falkirk. The area, long disputed, eventually became the northern boundary of the Kingdom of Northumbria which was dominated in turn by Angles, Danes and Saxons. Lothian is derived from the Saxon word *lothing*, meaning 'border'.

As with so many of the important places in Scottish history

it was King David I (1124–53) who first brought Linlithgow to prominence. He erected a manor house roughly where the present palace is now situated and, next to it, he built the Church of St Michael. The palace, now in ruins, was constructed much later by a succession of Stewart kings.

Due to Linlithgow's geographical location midway between Edinburgh and Stirling and only four miles from Blackness harbour on the River Forth, it was of great importance as a fortress and the area was known as Scotland's battlefield.

In 1301 Edward I of England took over the occupancy of the royal manor house and set about building a heavily fortified castle around it. This castle was held by the English during the remainder of the Scottish Wars of Independence but was liberated for Scotland in the autumn of 1313.

Linlithgow, along with its castle and church, continued to suffer badly at the hands of the English and in the first quarter of the fifteenth century was twice destroyed by fire, in 1411 and 1424. In 1425, King James I, who had recently returned from a long captivity in England, set about having the castle

Linlithgow Palace

rebuilt. This work took 12 years to complete and the ruins are still visible today.

Over the next few centuries the ruling members of the Stewart Dynasty added to the palace's dimensions. Linlithgow Palace played a very important part in the events that shaped Scottish history: James V and Mary Queen of Scots were born there; Oliver Cromwell spent the winter of 1650 in the palace after defeating the Scots army at Dunbar; Charles Edward Stuart stayed in the palace in 1745 when, allegedly, the fountain

Invasion by Roundheads

in the courtyard flowed with wine. In 1746 the palace was burned out by a detachment of the Duke of Cumberland's army under General Hawley who had been billeted there overnight on their way to Culloden.

The town was famed for its leather, weaving and dying industries with much of the shoes and cloth produced being sent to Europe through the port of Blackness close by. With the advent of first the Union Canal, followed by the Edinburgh to Glasgow Railway, the town's market became much more Scottish based.

After leaving Linlithgow the canal continues for another three miles to Philpstoun from where a short distance takes it to Winchburgh.

The canal between Philpstoun and Niddry is deep cut, sometimes as much as 20m high and represents a major piece of engineering, especially since it was constructed by hundreds of 'navvies' or navigators with nothing more than pick and shovel.

The most notorious of these navvies were William Burke and William Hare who, having come over from Ireland, stayed on to start their infamous bodysnatching business in Edinburgh.

From Winchburgh the canal snakes its way between several bings, remnants of the shale oil industry's claim in this area, and passes Niddry Castle beyond the Edinburgh to Glasgow Railway which runs parallel to the canal for most of the latter's length.

Until recently, Niddry Castle was a ruin, but in 1984 work was started to restore it to a habitable dwelling. The castle was built at the end of the fifteenth century by the Seaton family whose daughter, Mary Seaton, was one of Mary Queen of Scots's four Marys. It was here that the former Queen took refuge during her flight from imprisonment in Loch Leven Castle to Hamilton Palace in 1568.

The canal soon turns south-west to Broxburn. Broxburn, which means Badger's Burn, was a small, mainly agricultural village on the Earl of Buchan's estate until the arrival of the

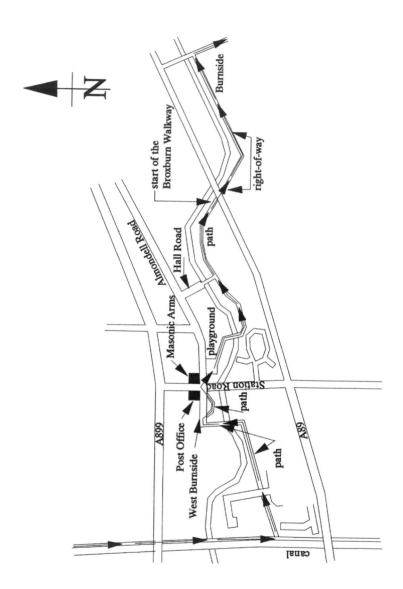

shale oil industry. The last of the oil works in the area closed in 1960.

The towpath is broken first by the B8020 (Greendykes Road) and then by the A899 West Main Street. A short distance later the canal is culverted under the M8 motorway a mile to the south. There are two ways to get round this impediment.

The first is to proceed along the towpath in a southerly direction until you can see a canal bridge ahead. About 100m before this bridge there is a rough path going through some bushes on the left. Take this path which, after a short distance, crosses Parkwood Gardens and continues on the other side. This is part of the Broxburn Walkway, a right-of-way which follows close to the Brox Burn as it runs through the town. It is 2½ miles long and finishes on the west side of Uphall. A leaflet which describes the length of this walkway is available from any West Lothian Council office.

Continue to follow this path as it runs adjacent to West Burnside, crosses Station Road, goes along Almondell Road for 20m and then passes through a children's playground, after which it follows the Brox Burn once again to finish at the A89. Cross this busy road and continue on along a right-of-way to a small collection of houses known as Burnside. Turn right here and follow this unclassified road for almost a mile, first crossing over the motorway then travelling under the Glasgow to Edinburgh Railway before reaching the canal once again.

The second route continues along the canal for a much longer distance before the deviation and does not go through Broxburn. After the canal towpath runs under the A89, it continues on for about half a mile to where an unclassified road passes over it. Here, although the towpath continues on, leave the canal and climb up on to this road. Turn right and follow it for a short distance until it meets a four-way junction. Just before this junction, on the right, there is a 100-foot circular entrenchment which is known as Roman Camp. Despite its name, this camp is Celtic and predates the Roman occupation by about a hundred years. At the crossroads turn left and follow this road for about a mile to Muirend. At this second

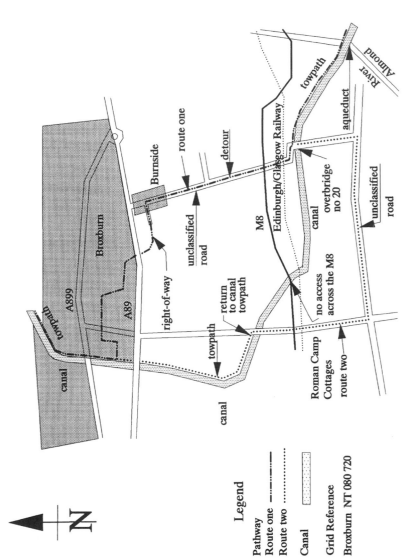

Legend

Pathway
Route one ─ ·─ ·─ ·─
Route two ·············

Canal

Grid Reference

Broxburn NT 080 720

N

Canal boat at Linlithgow

crossroads, turn left again. This minor road continues for a short distance to where it crosses over the top of the canal. At this point the traveller should rejoin the towpath heading east towards Edinburgh.

Once back on the canal towpath it's less than half a mile to the Almond Aqueduct. This five-span aqueduct is the smallest of the three major structures, with a span of about 500ft taking the canal high over the river. In the book, *The Union Canal: A Capital Asset*, by Guthrie Hutton, there is a photograph of the famous Broxburn Icicle. This icicle was formed during the intensely cold winter of 1895 and hung in its suspended magnificence from the overflow sluice at the top of the aqueduct, all the way to the river below. As Mr Hutton

Canal boats at the Bridge Inn, Ratho

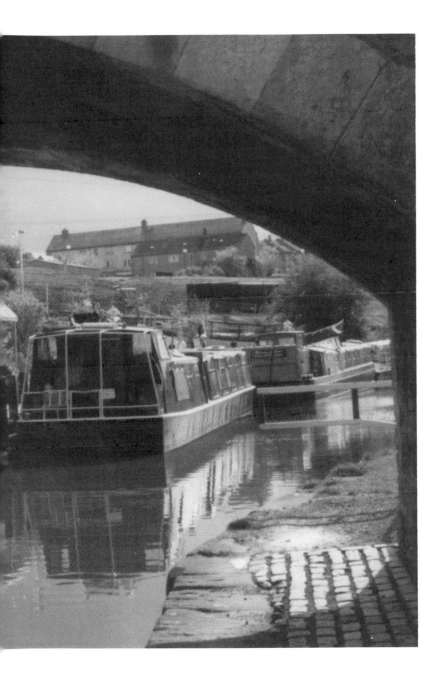

also reminds us, it was here at the adjacent Lin's Mill in 1645 that the luckless William Lin died; the last person in Scotland to die of bubonic plague.

After passing the second of these three great aqueducts you will discover the inlet of one of the main feeder-streams which tops up the canal's water level. As part of the canal project Cobbinshaw Reservoir was constructed some ten miles to the south in the hills above West Calder. It was built to prevent the water stocks of the Almond River from being depleted by the canal which would have stopped the many mills in existence on the river at that time from operating.

Except for where the towpath comes to within a few metres of the M8 motorway it follows a wooded route for much of the two miles to Ratho.

Just before Ratho is reached a new building can be seen on the opposite bank. This is a new boat house, built on the former Wilkie's Basin and belonging to the Sea Gull Trust who operate specially adapted canal boats for handicapped people.

The Bridge Inn is also on the opposite bank, just next to the road bridge which takes the B7030 over the canal. This excellent hostelry has a restaurant and bar and is well worth a visit. The proprietor takes the inn's canal heritage very seriously and has a fine collection of old photographs and memorabilia displayed around the walls.

Today Ratho is very much a dormitory village for Edinburgh with many new housing estates, but the old village owes its existence to the canal, and at the end of the nineteenth century had the dubious reputation of supporting 14 public houses. Its wide basin and wharf was a staging post for the many barges which plied up and down the canal with their varied cargoes.

The canal continues on from Ratho for three-and-a-half miles or so, travelling through wooded glade and gently rolling agricultural land and passing Ratho Park Golf Club on the opposite bank. Eventually, after crossing over the large modern aqueduct carrying the canal over the A720 Edinburgh Bypass, which is the first canal aqueduct to be built in

Scotland for over 150 years, the walkway ends abruptly at Wester Hailes.

Wester Hailes is a modern housing estate which has to be negotiated before the canal resumes again. It was built between 1969 and 1975 when the Housing Department considered that since the canal performed no useful function and would never do so again they would pipe it underground, therefore creating more space for the housing estate.

Edinburgh Canal Society's boathouse

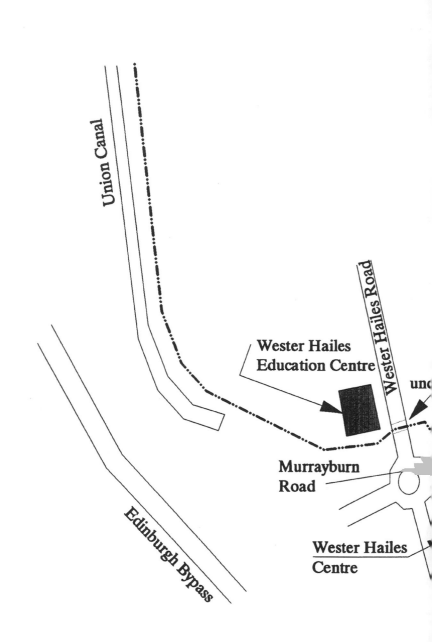

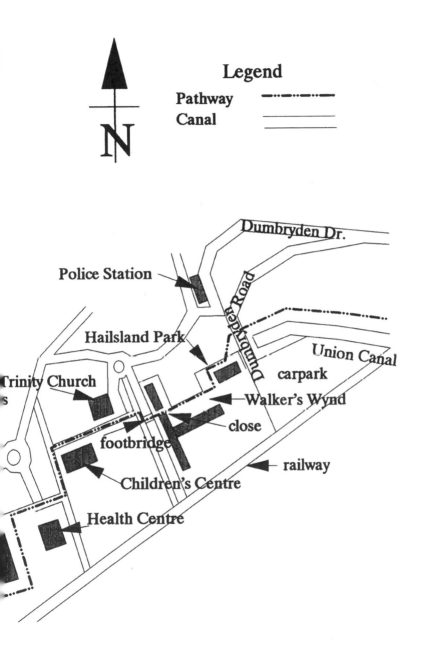

Legend
Pathway
Canal

Dumbryden Dr.
Police Station
Dumbryden Road
Hailsland Park
Union Canal
Trinity Church
carpark
Walker's Wynd
close
footbridge
railway
Children's Centre
Health Centre

On leaving the towpath continue in the same direction past some playing-fields, keeping them on your left, and within a short distance you will arrive at the gate of Wester Hailes Education Centre. Turn right out of the gates and go along the underpass which runs under Wester Hailes Road. On the other side of the underpass turn right up the hill and go through another underpass which leads to a piazza at the front of the Wester Hailes Centre. From here, either circumvent the four sides of this centre, starting up the ramp to the right of it, or go through it if it's open! Either way, join another piazza at the east end of the centre where a series of unnamed off-road footpaths commence.

Walk east through this pedestrian area, keeping to the left of the health centre, to arrive at a T-junction. Turn left at this junction and then take the first right past the children's centre to another T-junction. Once again, turn right then go left across a footbridge over Clovestone Road and through a close into Walker's Wynd.

After Walker's Wynd the route continues along Hailesland Park following below a strange, steel-clad multi-storey block to a path which leads up to Dumbryden Road. Cross this road to where the canal re-emerges and the towpath once again continues east passing Hailes Park which was the site of Hailes Quarry where whinstone was quarried for pavements and flagstones.

Travel on now to Slateford where the last two of the many aqueducts are located. The first, at Slateford, is the last of the three large multi-span structures which were built as part of the original canal. The second is known as Prince Charlie's aqueduct. This is a fairly modern structure having been rebuilt in 1937 when Slateford Road was widened. The name comes from the legend that Bonnie Prince Charlie stayed at Graysmill Farm House the night before he and his army of Highlanders entered Edinburgh in 1745. This farmhouse would have been located near where Inglis Green Road joins Slateford Road.

On the eastern end of this aqueduct is an access down on

to Slateford Road where the connection to the Water of Leith Walkway can be found close by.

The canal is very well used here by walkers, runners and cyclists. There are many boat and canoe clubs using the water, indeed the St Andrews Boat Club have been rowing here since 1846.

The canal runs east past Meggatland where Boroughmuir Rugby Club, one of Edinburgh's consistent premier league clubs, have their playing fields. Then it continues on another short distance to Edinburgh Canal Society's Boat House, on the opposite bank, at Ashley Terrace.

Within a very short distance the traveller passes Harrison Park and then Leamington Road lifting-bridge. This unique electrically operated lifting-bridge was moved to its present location, from Fountainbridge Road, in 1922 when the ports of Hopetoun and Hamilton were closed.

The canal ends in Fountainbridge just before Gilmore Park and, although at this point it is only a stone's-throw from the heart of the city, the canal is now teeming with many varieties of wildlife. Within 200m of Leamington Road lifting-bridge, I have seen breeding pairs of swans, ducks and moorhens, all nesting in the reeds and on the bank opposite the towpath.

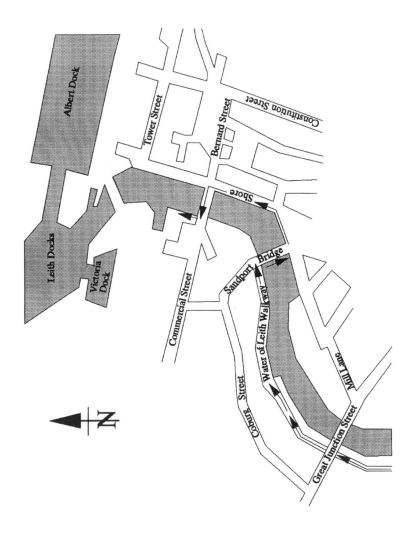

CHAPTER FIVE

Scenic Walks in Edinburgh

The Water of Leith Walkway

This route begins at Balerno. Enter Balerno from Lanark Road West into Bridge Road and carry along this for 100m or so to where the signposted Water of Leith path begins on the left. This 13½-mile-long, well-defined path will take you not only into the heart of Edinburgh but also to the ancient port of Leith.

After about a quarter of a mile you will reach the village of Currie which has a long milling history. From as far back as the sixteenth century, flax, snuff, paper and grain were produced here.

The village is situated almost entirely on the other side of Lanark Road and the footpath, which is on the north side of the river, is still surrounded by picturesque woodland. Soon, however, the walkway crosses to the south side of the Water of Leith. The ruins of Lennox Tower can be seen on the north bank. Thought to have been built in the sixteenth century by the Earl of Lennox, the brother of Lord Darnley, it is also believed that Mary Queen of Scots stayed here. This is all speculation, though, and there seems to be no existing record of the royal connections.

The route then passes Currie kirk which was dedicated, in

75

Currie kirk

the thirteenth century, to St Kentigern (St Mungo), the patron
saint of Glasgow. The present kirk dates from 1785. A mort-
safe can still be seen here, a chilling reminder of Messrs Burke
and Hare, the bodysnatchers. Robert Louis Stevenson spent
many of his boyhood days here at the manse — his maternal
grandfather, the Revd Lewis Balfour, was the minister.

After passing the adjoining village of Juniper Green, the
walkway passes under the huge road bridge, which takes the
City of Edinburgh Bypass high above the river valley, before
winding its way onward to Spylaw Park.

From the north side of the park the path comes out into

Colinton Village. The history of the village of Colinton is recorded as far back as 1095, when Ethelred, second son of Malcolm Canmore, gifted the lands known as 'Halis' to the church of the Holy Trinity in Dunfermline. There has been a village here for many hundreds of years clustered around Colinton parish church and its churchyard.

Up until now the route has travelled along the disused Slateford to Balerno branch railway line, and after passing Colinton it enters the 300-yard-long railway tunnel. Once through this tunnel, the path descends into a very beautiful and spectacular gorge known as Colinton Dell. On the other side of the dell the walkway ends temporarily when it joins Lanark Road at a hostelry called the Tickled Trout.

You have now arrived in Slateford, another of Edinburgh's old villages. As its name suggests, it was known as a place to ford the river. Slate was a reference to the local stone mined here. The village became part of Edinburgh in 1920. To the north is the viaduct built in 1847 by the Caledonian Railway Company and the aqueduct which carries the Union Canal. A little way down Lanark Road are the remains of the old village, most of which was demolished during a road-widening scheme in 1964. These are Slateford House and The Cross Keys, an old eighteenth-century coaching inn. Behind them is the old secession church and manse. Directly across the road from the Tickled Trout is the old school, built in 1864 and now home to the Water of Leith Heritage Centre, which is well worth a visit.

After leaving the Heritage Centre, head south for a short distance to Inglis Green Road. Here turn right and follow this road to a close known as 'The Burnside' which is beside a pub called The Longstone Inn. Go through this close and follow the walkway around the perimeter fence of Saughton Prison; the full extent of the grim rear edifice is visible.

Travel along Stenhouse Mill Lane to where Stenhouse Castle, as it is known locally, is found. The 'castle' was once known as Stanhope House after the family who owned it, but this name has evolved over the centuries to 'Stenhouse', which is now also the name of the district. Originally built for the Abbot of Holyrood, it was taken over by Patrick Ellis, an Edinburgh merchant, who had the house extended in 1623; it is his coat-of-arms which can be seen over the front door.

Cross Gorgie Road, turn right and go on a short distance to where the Water of Leith flows under the road. Here turn left and follow the footpath to Fords Road where the walkway continues into Saughton Park on the opposite side of the road.

Water of Leith Heritage Centre, Slateford

Saughton Park was originally the grounds of Saughton House until the first years of the twentieth century when it was bought over by Edinburgh Corporation to house the Scottish National Exhibition of 1908. Since then it has remained a public park. In 1952 Saughton House was dramatically burned down by Edinburgh Corporation in a controlled fire supervised by the Fire Brigade — the house was so riddled with rot that burning was the only way to demolish it safely.

Leave the park at Balgreen Road. Cross this road and follow the walkway as it continues by the banks of the river to a footbridge at Baird Drive. Cross this footbridge and follow the path as it passes the Edinburgh Ice Rink which was built on the site of Dalry Mill, the first paper-mill on the river. Further on, the path also passes close to Murrayfield Stadium, the home of international rugby in Scotland. Work has recently been completed to rebuild the main stand and create new stands, making this an all-seater stadium which many believe to be the best in the country. Let's hope the new stadium sees as many great victories for Scotland's rugby team as did its predecessor, which was first built on this site in 1925. When the foundations of the original stadium were being excavated, a coffin was discovered. It contained the body of a soldier who still had his musket; he was probably a trooper in Cromwell's army, who were encamped here in 1650.

Enter Roseburn Park and carry on to Roseburn Place, then turn left into Rose Gardens. At the end of this street is Roseburn Terrace. Cross this busy road and continue in an easterly direction to the Roseburn to Granton Cycleway, first passing under the railway bridge (now painted in its smart Caledonian Railway colours, with the company crest displayed in the centre). Under this bridge there is a milestone declaring that it is '1 mile to Edinburgh and 41 to Glasgow'.

At the east end of the bridge, just around the corner, is the access up to cycleway. Continue in the direction of Granton for a few hundred metres to where a set of 86 steps leads you down from the top of Coltbridge Railway Viaduct to the Water of Leith Walkway. Continue along this walkway, passing another footbridge which connects with a path up to the Scottish National Gallery of Modern Art.

This area is known as Coltbridge. An alluvial basin, it once contained a notorious bog which caused many problems for people travelling from Edinburgh to Corstorphine, then a village on the city outskirts. It was also the place where, in September 1745, two regiments of government dragoons which had been left behind to protect Edinburgh while the rest of Sir John Cope's army marched north, were routed by Bonnie Prince Charlie's invading Highlanders, thus leaving the city undefended. The next day Charles Edward Stewart entered the city in triumph.

Soon the path crosses the river by a footbridge and continues through picturesque woodland, which is surprising to find in the middle of a city.

At this point the river is at its broadest as it cascades over the West Mill Weir. Here Edinburgh District Council must take credit for a fine piece of civil engineering with the ramp which takes the walkway up and over the top of the weir.

The path now enters Dean Valley and follows a particularly beautiful route, passing first West Mill, recently restored as a block of flats, and then the Edinburgh Hilton Hotel, which is on the site of Bell's Mill. Continue under Belford Bridge to reach Dean Village.

Dean Village was originally called the Village of the Water of Leith. Though fairly close, it was quite separate from the Village of Dean. The latter no longer exists, and today's Dean Village is still seen quite clearly as a self-contained village, despite being right in the heart of the city. This is because of its unique location, set as it is below the level of the busy streets of the New Town with the traffic crossing high above on Telford's Bridge. In the village there is a sense of going back in time, of joining another world.

The village was once dominated by its many mills. Indeed, milling has been an important industry here since the twelfth century. At one time there were 11 mills in or close to the village, run for the most part by the Incorporation of Baxters (the Scots version of the Guild of Bakers). The 'Mills of Dene' were referred to in the Charter to Holyrood Abbey where King David I gave the Augustinian Friars the ownership of the mills on the Water of Leith.

Until the 1960s the village had been in a state of steady decline, with many of the houses falling into disrepair. In the last 30 years or so, however, there has been a renaissance. Today it is much rejuvenated and many of its buildings have been extremely well restored. The general picture portrayed by the village is one of tranquil beauty.

Stanhope House

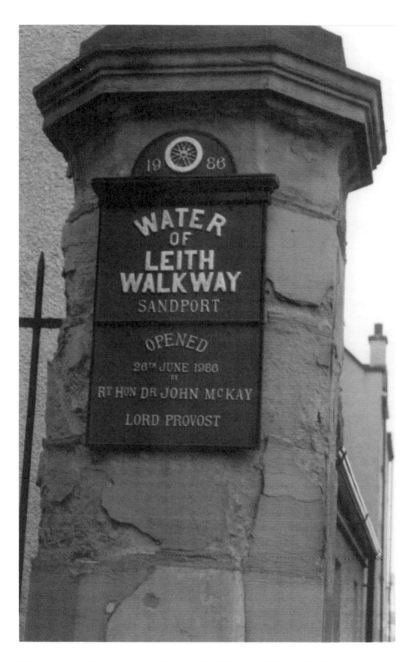

Plaque marking the opening of the Water of Leith Walkway

Cross the river via the footbridge and follow the path as it continues to Hawthorn Bank, crosses Dean Path and joins Miller Row on the other side. Fairly soon you will see Thomas Telford's magnificent bridge which spans this deep river gorge at a height of 106ft. Continue on under Telford Bridge.

The path follows the river downstream, passing another quaint little building. This is St George's Well, which was built in 1810 as rival to its neighbour, St Bernard's Well.

Much has been written about St Bernard's Well recently and possibly the most complete account, written by Neil Macara Brown, can be found in an Edinburgh District Council brochure. Published to celebrate the bicentenary of the building of the existing well house in 1789 and the centenary of its restoration in 1888, the brochure is widely available throughout the city free of charge. Legend has it that St Bernard of Clairvaux, founder of the Cistercian Order, came to Scotland to recruit soldiers for the Second Crusade. During this time he became ill and retired to a cave close to where the Dean Bridge is situated today. He found a spring close by and drank its healing waters until his strength returned. The spring was rediscovered in 1760 by three boys out fishing on the Water of Leith. An analysis was made of the water and it was found to be similar to the sulphur springs at Harrogate in Yorkshire. This event led to Stockbridge becoming a spa for the taking of the waters.

Travel on now through very pleasant gardens to Stockbridge. One of Edinburgh's oldest villages, for many hundreds of years Stockbridge was a fording point for the Water of Leith, which in those days was much wider than it is today. There was also a footbridge for pedestrians at the same point. The first stone bridge was erected here in 1785 and was widened in 1820. This is the bridge which still exists today and is simply called Stockbridge. Looking at the small stream which is now the Water of Leith, it may be hard to believe that it was once a wide, fast-flowing river. Indeed, many times in the last few centuries, it turned into a raging torrent following long periods of persistent rain, flooding the surrounding streets causing damage to property and severe discomfort to local people. The worst flood of all was recorded in 1659 when 16 mills were destroyed by the surging mass of water. In 1885 all the old mill lades were removed by Edinburgh Corporation; high river walls were erected in their place to retain the surrounding streets in the way that can be seen today.

Stockbridge is renowned as the home of two of Scotland''s most famous artists. The celebrated portrait painter Henry Raeburn was born in the village in 1756, and David Roberts was born there in 1796. Roberts' house, called 'Duncan's Land', now a restaurant, is in nearby Gloucester Street.

At the end of these gardens continue through the archway into Saunders Street, at the end of which is Deanhaugh Street. Cross this street and turn left. Continue for a short distance to where a flight of stone stairs descends to Deanhaugh path which runs along the west bank of the river.

Travel on for some 200m to St Bernard's Row where the path temporarily ends. Continue on by way of Arboretum Avenue to reach Rocheid Path where the river path recommences. On the other side of the river, crossed by a footbridge, is an area known as the Colonies. The houses there, terraces of symmetrical cottages, were built by the Co-operative Movement between 1861 and 1911 for working-class families to buy at low cost. Today they are much sought-after and are very expensive.

Go on into Inverleith Terrace Lane, at the end of which is Inverleith Row. Cross this road and head south for a short distance to Warriston Crescent.

If you carry on a bit further before leaving Inverleith Row, you will come to the East Gate entrance of the Edinburgh Royal Botanic Garden. This is the second-oldest botanic garden in Britain. It was originally started as a Physic Garden in 1667 by Dr Robert Sibbald and Dr Robert Balfour and was located on a small site close to Holyrood Abbey. (Sibbald went on to found the Royal College of Physicians in 1681.) It eventually settled in its present 72-acre site in Inverleith in 1820. The Garden attracts many thousands of tourists each year. Amongst many other magnificent treasures, the Garden has perhaps the world's greatest collection of Vireya Rhododendrons, with almost a hundred varieties displayed. It has 11 wonderful plant-houses known collectively, these days, as the 'Glasshouse Experience', which contain plants from every climatic region of the world. There is also a great deal of scientific research and conservation work done there.

Once you reach Warriston Crescent, try to find number 10 where there is a plaque. It reads: Fredrick Chopin (1810 to 1849), Polish Composer, stayed here on the occasion of his Scottish concert in Edinburgh on the 4th of October 1848.

At the end of Warriston Crescent the route continues between two high fences until it reaches a bridge over the Water of Leith. Cross this and climb up a short flight of wooden stairs and turn left to join the Leith to Broughton Road Cycleway. If you now turn right, you will reach Broughton Road, only a quarter of a mile away.

If, however, you carry on in a north easterly direction towards Leith, you will soon pass over an old stone bridge which takes the cycletrack over the Warriston Cemetery.

Continue on for about 300m to find a gap in the fence on the right. Go through this gap to meet Warriston Road, here again the walkway and the cycle track split up. However, if you were to stay on the cycle route, it will merge again with the walkway at Stedfastgate.

Take the path to the right and follow the road downhill to reach a bridge over the river. Turn left, going down a few stairs as the path continues alongside St Marks Park. Powderhall greyhound stadium is on the other side of the river. Follow this path on through an underpass under a railway. Soon you will come across a ruined mill — traces of the mill lade are still clearly defined. This is the first of the 71 mills (which haven't totally disappeared) of the Water of Leith. You will also see the weir built for the mill which clearly shows how wide the river once was.

After a short distance the walkway and cycle route once

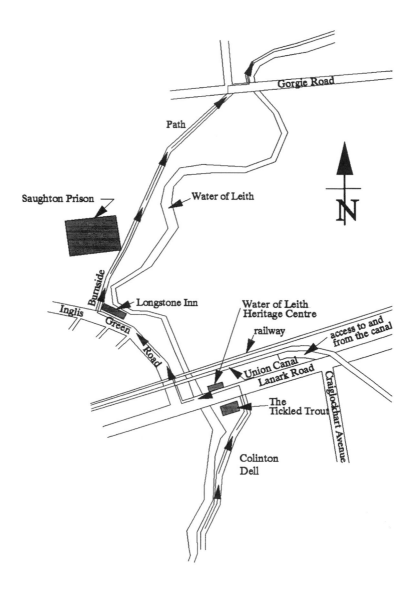

again meet at Stedfastgate. There is a monument here to mark the centenary of the Leith Battalion of the Boys Brigade. The monument is named after the BB's motto, 'Sure and Steadfast', and was built with stones from the Catherine Sinclair fountain which stood at the junction of Princes Street and Lothian Road until 1932. At that time it was put in store until the 1980s when it was erected once again in its present position.

This shared path continues another half-mile or so to Sandford Bridge in Leith where the walkway and the cycle route end. Some old street rhymes, such as the one below, can be seen on the paving-stones:

> At different stages o' erection
> The very essence o' perfection
> There's no sicht can turn aside
> The bias o' shipbuilders' pride.

This dual walkway and cycleway is, for once, a testament to good planning. Before the walkway was built, the area along the adjacent riverbanks was in a terrible state of industrial decline and neglect. The walkway has transformed the northern riverbank into a pleasant area equally suitable both for leisure and recreation and for commuter cycling to and from Edinburgh. Built to a very high standard, it has a smooth, even surface along the whole of its length. More importantly, the cycleway is lit, allowing it to be used at night or during the winter.

The port of Leith was granted to the Burgh of Edinburgh by King Robert I (the Bruce) in 1329, inevitably starting a quarrel between the burgesses of Edinburgh and the people of Leith. The bad feeling endured until 1838, when a City Agreement Act made Leith became a separate municipality. The town was finally merged with the capital in 1920 as part of the Edinburgh Boundaries Extension Act.

Leith's harbour has always been the linchpin of the town's prosperity and this is one of the main reasons behind the long, bitter struggle with Edinburgh — which some Leithers would say is still going on to this day. In medieval times Royal Burghs

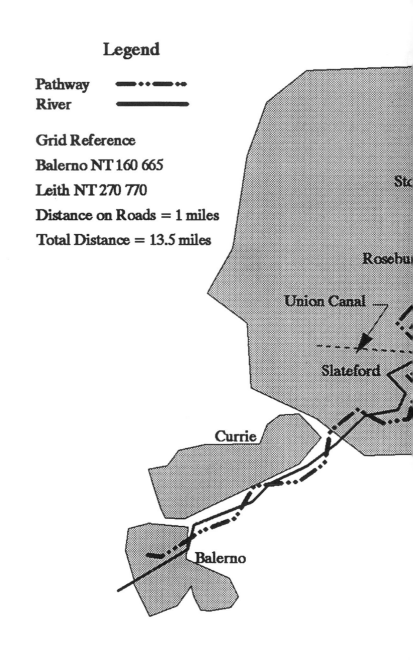

Legend

Pathway

River

Grid Reference

Balerno NT 160 665

Leith NT 270 770

Distance on Roads = 1 miles

Total Distance = 13.5 miles

St...

Rosebu...

Union Canal

Slateford

Currie

Balerno

(such as Edinburgh) had the exclusive right to trade abroad; as Leith was not a Royal Burgh, the local merchants were legally excluded from importing or exporting goods. They were expected to stand by and watch their neighbours from Edinburgh monopolise this lucrative trade. Needless to say, many Leith merchants refused to obey these rules and struck up links with the profitable foreign markets, thereby risking imprisonment by the king.

In the early years of the sixteenth century the people of Leith's problems were exacerbated by the arrival of merchants from Aberdeen who, as a result of their own port's decline, were forced south to Leith to trade. Indeed, at this time, the burgesses of Edinburgh purchased from King James IV the adjacent port at Newhaven in a bid to enlarge the area's harbour facilities. These events did nothing to help the frustrations of the local people.

In 1544 the English Army landed at the port in an attempt to launch an attack on Edinburgh. Under the command of the Earl of Hertford, the English soldiers seized two ships and, in the affray that followed, many men of the local Leith militia were killed defending their town. After sacking and burning Leith, the soldiers marched on Edinburgh. Here, though, they encountered fierce resistance, forcing them back to England but they destroyed everything in their path as they retreated south. This was the beginning of the so-called 'Rough Wooing' by Henry VIII.

In 1571, while the civil war raged, noblemen loyal to the now exiled Mary Queen of Scots still retained their control over the Parliament in Edinburgh. An opposing Parliament was set up in the town of Leith by supporters of Mary's son, who had been crowned King James VI when his mother had fled to England three years earlier after the Battle of Langside. This situation led to the 'Leith Settlement' which was concluded by representatives of the Kirk and members of the privy council. However, it did little to ease the divisions within the country.

In 1645 the bubonic plague ravaged many of the towns on the East Coast of Scotland, particularly affecting the luckless

Leith, where the disease cost the lives of at least half the population. This poor fortune was to continue five years later when the town was occupied by a large garrison of Cromwell's army.

There are positive aspects to the town's history as well. Leith is very important in the development of the game of golf — in fact, the first historical reference to the game was made by James II in 1457 when he banned golf from Leith Links because it was interfering with the army's archery practice. The original 13 rules of golf were also drawn up in Leith in 1744.

Until the middle of the nineteenth century the port was one of Scotland's foremost shipbuilding centres. The SS *Sirius*, the first steam-ship to cross the Atlantic, was built there in 1837. Its dry dock, dating from 1720, was the first ever to be built in Scotland. When much larger iron and steel vessels were needed, though, the shipyards' shallow water was unable to cope and the industry dwindled to a fraction of its former glory. The remaining yards concentrated on the building of specialised craft; in 1944, for example, much of the Mulberry Harbour used in the D-Day landings in France was assembled in great secrecy here.

Leith is now renowned as a gourmet centre with many fine restaurants in the town.

The Roseburn to Cramond Cycleway

The route begins at Dalry Road at Muirieston Crescent. An on-street cycle route is clearly signposted to where the railway cycle track begins at Russell Road close to Murrayfield Stadium. This route follows the line of the Granton, Leith and Barnton branch railway (off the main Carstairs—Edinburgh line), which was opened by the Caledonian Railway Company in 1861.

The branch has an interesting history. It went as far as Granton harbour, which had been built by the Duke of Buccleuch in 1855 to compete with the nearby ports of

Newhaven and Leith. The railway was principally intended to carry coal and other freight to the harbour, for onward carriage by sea, but three years later a branch line was opened to Leith Station. In 1879 passenger services were started from Lothian Road to Leith and in 1894 a further branch line was opened to carry passengers to the new residential areas of Davidson's Mains and Barnton. The railway was closed in stages between 1951 and 1986 when the lines were dismantled.

Just after the start at Russell Road the railway path crosses the bridge over Roseburn Terrace. The cycle route shares this path with the Water of Leith Walkway and the bridge and surrounding area has already been described above. If you look over the bridge east towards Edinburgh there is a row of cottages next to the bridge on the north side of the road. They were built by the Caledonian Railway Company for their employees. On the other side of the road is an area known as Coates where the directors and managers of the company lived.

After passing Coltbridge railway viaduct and the steps down to the Water of Leith Walkway below, the cycleway passes under Upper Coltbridge Terrace where the Gallery of Modern Art is located. A mile further on, the cycleway passes the platform of Craigleith Station and goes on under Craigleith Road, part of the A90, which is the main road to the Forth Bridge and the north. Just past this to the east of the path is a supermarket. It was built on the site of Craigleith Quarry which supplied the stone for the Usher Hall, most of the grand houses of the New Town, and even Buckingham Palace in London. This is also the spot where the Barnton branch line leaves the main route and goes off in a westerly direction. Today it is used as the cycle route to Davidson's Mains, ending at Silverknowes Road East.

Continue on another half-mile or so to the bridge over Ferry Road; immediately beyond this the cycleway bisects once again. Nearby is one of the area's biggest employers, GEC Marconi (formally Ferranti), who make vital components for guided missiles. Take the route to the left unless you want to go to Granton Road (where the cycle track finishes) or on to Leith using the dismantled railway solum. (This cycle path is scheduled to be extended to join the Warriston Walkway.)

The route to the left is the cycle path which was constructed by Spokes. It finishes just north of West Granton Road where it joins Caroline Park Avenue. Here the railway solum (which at present is perfectly good to walk on) will be upgraded to extend the cycle route to Granton harbour. From there it is possible to get a ferry to Burntisland in Fife. This very quiet, narrow road has been blocked off to vehicles at its north end, at West Shore Road, Granton, making it perfectly safe for cycling or walking.

When West Shore Road is reached, cross to the other side and turn left. Within 100m, a wide tarmac path once more begins in the direction of the shore. This is the beginning of the promenade which will take you the remaining 5km to Cramond. On a clear day many of the islands in the Firth of Forth can be seen, including Inchmickery, Inchcolm and, of course, the closest of all, Cramond Island.

Halfway between Granton and Cramond a large house is visible at the top of the escarpment. This is Craigcrook Castle, which was built as a keep in 1545 by Bailie Adamson, Guardian of Edinburgh, for the defence and provision of Edinburgh in the event of a siege. The castle has been extended many times by its numerous owners, one of whom was Francis Jeffrey, friend of Sir Walter Scott and founder of the famous literary magazine, *The Edinburgh Review*. Until recently, the house was the offices of a firm of architects.

On now to the ancient village of Cramond. Its name was originally spelt Caer Almond in Roman times, and meant simply 'the fort on the mouth of the river Almond', which is exactly what it was. Just before the promenade turns along the riverside, a large tower-house can be seen off to the left. This is Cramond Tower. Not much is known about its origins, but it was renovated recently and is now used as a private residence. In AD142 engineers of the Roman Army chose this spot to build a harbour and fort to service the construction of

Antonine's Wall. It would seem that the local tribe, a branch of the North British known as the Gododdin (called the Votadini by the Romans), were well disposed to the Roman presence here and actively traded with them and assisted them in the building of the fort.

Excavated by archaeologists in 1954, the fort was very large and covered an area measuring six acres. Made of clay and stone, it was rectangular and had towers at each corner, four gates and 20-foot-high walls which were 27 feet thick. A model and the major finds of the excavation are kept in the Huntley House Museum in the Canongate and a plan of part of the structure can be seen on the site of the fort next to Cramond kirk.

A village grew up around the fort's east rampart. The people grew oats and barley and herded pigs which they traded with the Roman soldiers, whose first occupation of the fort lasted about 12 years. This was followed by a second occupation which lasted for a shorter period of time. The third and final time the Romans took over the fort was during the reign of the Emperor Septimus Severus, who refurbished it during his campaign in Caledonia between AD208 and AD211. Although the Roman presence in this area was of brief duration, it had a profound effect on the Gododdin. Long after the Romans had left the area, the tribespeople continued to live in the fort, making repairs and even carrying out new building work in the Roman style. Roman pottery dating from the fourth century AD has been found there which would suggest that the local people traded with the Romans in the south. The Gododdin also seem to have embraced the Christian religion, for they used the basilica within the Principia of the fort as a place of worship. Around AD600, when they decided to build the first of their own churches, it was constructed with stone from the Principia in the same location. Cramond kirk stands on the spot today.

Also around AD600, the Gododdin King, Mynyddog, moved his tribe's headquarters to Din Eidyn (Dun Edin), which is Edinburgh Castle Rock. The reason for this move north was probably because, with the Romans gone, the Gododdin were being threatened by a new enemy from the south in the form of the Angles of Northumbria. Fearful of being overrun, King Mynyddog sent an army south, but it was heavily defeated and by the middle of the seventh century the Angles were firmly in control of the area around Midlothian.

Cramond village and its little church survived. At various times throughout its long history the church has been added to, the most recent work being done in 1955. Although other villages around the area (such as Muttonhole, Davidson's Mains, on the crossroads between Edinburgh, Leith, Queensferry and Cramond) became more important as time went on, nothing much has happened to Cramond over the centuries.

Thanks to the deep gorge and fast-flowing water along the banks of the River Almond, the iron-milling industry grew up in the seventeenth and eighteenth centuries. In the early part of the 1700s four mills worked side by side between the village and Old Cramond Brig, barely a mile upstream. The ruins of Fairafar Mill can still be seen today.

In Victorian times Cramond and its environs became popular as the summer home of Edinburgh's well-to-do residents. In 1860 Queen Victoria visited Cramond twice, staying at Cramond House, which was built by John Inglis in 1680 and owned by Lady Torphichen. Today this delightful village has lost none of its character and is a pleasant spot for a refreshing walk and a breath of sea air.

Cramond to South Queensferry via the Almond Ferry

The Almond Ferry, nothing more than a rowing-boat, is located near to where the river joins the Firth of Forth. It operates between 9 a.m. and 7 p.m. April to September, and between 10 a.m. and 4 p.m. October to March. The adult fare is 50p, children 10p; children under six go free. It stops for an hour between 1 and 2 p.m. and is closed all day Friday. The ferry will not carry dogs (they are not allowed into Dalmeny Estate, as it is a bird sanctuary), prams or bicycles.

The path from the west bank of the Almond passes through the Dalmeny Estate which belongs to the Earl of Rosebery. This is private land, so please respect the rules. Picnics are prohibited within the estate and visitors are requested to keep to the prescribed paths. Having said all this, the walk is still a very interesting and exciting one — well worth doing.

The route is a little under five miles long and is clearly signposted along its length. The first stretch follows a more or less coastal route and passes Eagle Rock, a huge sculptured rock which has the Imperial Eagle of Rome inscribed upon it. Continue along the coastal path for a further mile and a half until Dalmeny House is reached. It was built in 1816 though the Primrose family, Earls of Rosebery, to whom it belongs, have lived on this estate for much longer — almost 350 years, in fact. The house is open to the public during the summer and has two fine collections of paintings and furniture.

The path follows the perimeter of Dalmeny golf course until it reaches the estate road. Follow this road for a time and you will soon pass Barnbougle Castle. Built in the traditional Scottish style with stepped gables, the castle was until recently a ruin. It was rebuilt by the Earl of Rosebery in the 1950s in its original style and today the castle is once again occupied.

A little further on the two roads split. Take the road to the right which follows the coast. The peace and tranquillity of your surroundings is only disturbed from time to time by pheasants scrambling through the undergrowth away from your oncoming feet.

On another mile or so to where the river and the path turn south-west. This is known as Hound Point. Close to the shore is the BP Oil Terminal where oil from the North Sea is transported by pipe to a storage area near the village of Dalmeny. From there it is pumped to the oil terminal for onward transportation by ship. Also at Hound Point you will get the first view of the two bridges across the Forth. As you head towards these magnificent monuments of nineteenth- and twentieth-century civil engineering, you could be forgiven for thinking they are only five minutes' walk away — their scale is such that, even though there is over a mile still to go, they totally dominate the skyline ahead.

The Forth Railway Bridge was completed in 1890. This multi-cantilever structure was built to carry the North British Railway line across the Firth of Forth. The 361ft-tall bridge was designed by architect Sir John Fowler and engineer Benjamin Baker. It is made up of 54,000 tons of steel, over 6 million rivets, 740,000 cubic feet of granite, 46,300 tons of rubble masonry and 21,000 tons of cement. The Tay Bridge had collapsed in a storm 11 years before and the designers were

Barnbougle Castle

97

very anxious to ensure their bridge did not suffer the same fate. The Forth Bridge was intended to carry much greater loads and before it was opened the structure was test-loaded to 1,800 tons by two special trains travelling over it simultaneously.

The Forth Road Bridge is a suspension bridge and was completed in 1964. This very slender structure is similar to that of its neighbour in that it is built entirely of structural steel, except for the reinforced concrete deck. This bridge was opened by the Queen on 4 September 1964, after which she and the Duke of Edinburgh were passengers on the Queen Margaret, the last ferry to cross the Firth of Forth. Today the traffic using this bridge has increased greatly since it was opened and some people think that a second road crossing should be built.

Nestling at the foot of the two bridges lies the ancient village of South Queensferry — or The Queen's Ferry as it was originally known. The name refers to Queen Margaret, wife of King Malcolm III, King of Scots. Margaret, a very pious person, encouraged her subjects to go on pilgrimages to St Andrews. To this end, she had houses-of-refuge built on either side of the Firth of Forth and a free boat to ferry the pilgrims back and forth. The Queen used this crossing many times herself.

Margaret's link with this area started much earlier. She was born in Hungary in 1046, the daughter of the exiled Saxon prince, Edward Atheling. At the age of 12 she and her family returned to England as guests of her father's uncle, Edward (Edward the Confessor). After the Norman Conquest of 1066, Margaret's brother Edgar, who was now the heir to Edward's throne (and the man the Saxon people wanted as king in preference to William the Conqueror), was finding life in Norman England increasingly dangerous. In 1068 he and his sister escaped. Their ship was blown off course in a storm and the couple found themselves in the Firth of Forth. They were invited by Malcolm Canmore to stay at his stronghold in Dunfermline. In 1070 Margaret was persuaded to marry Malcolm, thus becoming his second wife — although she had wished to take up a monastic life. She bore Malcolm six sons (three of whom were to become kings of Scotland) but still found time for tireless work amongst the poor, reorganising the Celtic Church and civilising life within the royal court. She died on 16 November 1093 and was canonised — Scotland's first and only royal saint — by Pope Innocent IV in 1249. To mark the 900th anniversary of her death, the ladies of St Margaret's Chapel Guild, an organisation founded over 50 years ago, and who are responsible for the flowers in St Margaret's Chapel within Edinburgh Castle, presented every female child born in Scotland on 16 November 1993 with a silver pendant in the shape of a Marguerite.

As you walk through the Dalmeny Estate between Cramond and South Queensferry, enjoying the peace and tranquillity of the scene both on shore and in the estuary, it may be hard to imagine the magnitude of what happened on these waters on 21 November 1918. For it was shortly after dawn on that morning that the German High Seas Fleet filed in through the billowing mist to begin their ignominious passage between the lines of the entire British Grand Fleet. The numbers of the largest fighting fleet in the world were further swollen that day by five huge American dreadnoughts, three Australian cruisers and a representative warship from France, Italy, and Japan — a total of 60 battleships and 120 light cruisers and destroyers. The German Fleet of 49 ships in all (it had been 50, but one torpedo-boat had struck a mine the previous evening and had sunk) was a sizable part of the second-largest fleet in the world.

As the German ships approached the mouth of the Firth of Forth, headed by the escort cruiser HMS *Cardiff*, they approached the two vast lines of waiting vessels who flanked them for the remainder of their journey. The commander-in-chief of the Allied Fleet, Admiral Beatty, gave the order to clear the decks for action and all 180 ships responded speedily. The German Fleet, headed by *Seiner Majestät Schiff Seydlitz*, a survivor of the Battle of Jutland, steamed between the threatening lines, with more than a thousand guns trained

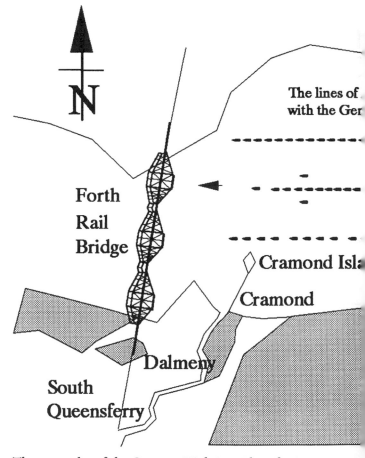

The lines of
with the Ger

Forth
Rail
Bridge

Cramond Isl

Cramond

Dalmeny

South
Queensferry

The surrender of the German High Seas Fleet, for internment,
the hands of the British Grand Fleet and other Allied ships i
Firth of Forth on 21 November 1918

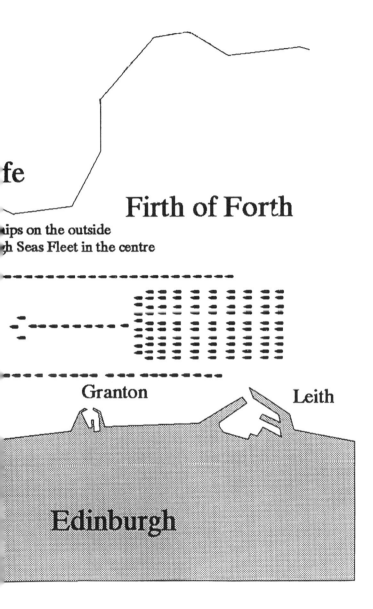

fe

Firth of Forth

ips on the outside
h Seas Fleet in the centre

Granton   Leith

Edinburgh

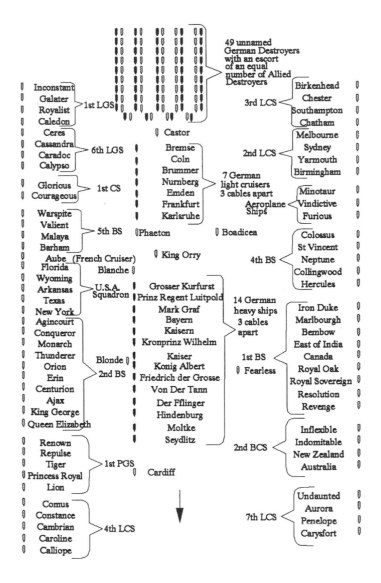

*The order of the British and German fleets in the Firth of Forth,
21 November 1918*

upon them in eerie silence. With the face of every allied sailor covered with a gas-mask, they watched the oncoming German ships. As part of the agreed armistice, the German Fleet was unarmed.

The curtain of fog was receding little by little with the rising sun and the spectacle was stupendous, even overpowering. As the wind blew over the vast number of ships in the Firth of Forth it bore with it a tremor of awe: world history was being made before the eyes of the watching thousands. All along the Firth of Forth, from Leith to Rosyth, people watched with great joy and boats of all shapes and sizes, packed with onlookers, began to crowd these waters. The Germans are beaten — the British Fleet has liberated the seas! This, of course, was not the case, for the German Fleet was undefeated. It was a political act which had brought it to Scotland that November day. In an uncoded wireless message from the British flagship HMS *Queen Elizabeth*, Admiral Beatty announced to the whole world: 'The German flag is to be hauled down at sunset [3.57 p.m.] and is not to be re-hoisted without permission.' So it was that at the appointed hour, with heavy heart, the order was given by Rear-Admiral Ludwig von Reuter from his flagship Friedrich der Grosse: 'Schleppen die Flagge abwärts — Haul down the flag.'

Two days later the fleet was escorted to Scapa Flow in Orkney where it was interned and, in a gesture of defiance and to restore self-respect, on 21 June 1919 the Germans scuttled their entire fleet.

Seventeen of the German ships were raised from the sea-bed at Scapa Flow and taken back to the Firth of Forth to be broken up at Rosyth. It is interesting to note that in the middle and late 1930s much of the salvaged steel was bought by Krupp of Essen to help build Hitler's new navy. One of the ships built by them was the Graf Spee which, of course, was scuttled outside Montevideo harbour after the Battle of the River Plate in 1939. Another interesting fact is that the salvage of this great fleet is still going on today, for this is the largest concentration of non-radioactive steel in the world — all steel manufactured after the Atom Bomb was dropped on Hiroshima contains a quantity of radiation. This uncontaminated steel is used in the production of very delicate scientific instruments both for medical purposes and the space industry.

There are many buildings and places of interest in South Queensferry, including the seventeenth-century Hawes Inn which featured in Robert Louis Stevenson's Kidnapped, and the Priory Church of St Mary of Mount Carmel which, now restored as the town's episcopal church, was once a Carmelite friary founded in 1441. The town is also endowed with a fine little museum, which is well worth a visit.

South Queensferry to Linlithgow via Bo'ness

After walking through South Queensferry from East to West, passing the museum in High Street, the route to Bo'ness starts at Hopetoun Road. At the point where the Bo'ness Road goes under the Forth Road Bridge, the pedestrian/cycle access across the bridge also begins. Follow the Hopetoun Road past Port Edgar for almost two miles until you reach Hopetoun Estate.

Port Edgar (called after St Margaret's brother) was constructed in 1870 by the North British Railway Company as a ferry terminal. However, their lack of forethought was demonstrated when, less than 20 years later, it became redundant when the rail bridge was completed. It was subsequently taken over by the Royal Navy and was used as a destroyer base in the First World War and a training base in the Second World War. The harbour was abandoned by the Navy in 1978 and today is used extensively as a yacht marina and a centre for water sports.

Hopetoun House, now the home of the Marquess of Linlithgow, was first built on this site in 1699 by the first Earl of Hopetoun, Charles Hope. The first house was designed by Sir William Bruce in a neoclassical and renaissance style but William Adam was commissioned in 1721 to make substantial alterations. These were not completed until almost 1770. This magnificent house contains portraits by David Allan, Allan Ramsay and Sir Henry Raeburn. Stretching all the way down to the Forth, the grounds of Hopetoun House are among the most beautiful in Scotland.

From the end of Hopetoun Road travel along the beach which boarders the estate for just over a mile to where the path through Wester Shore Wood begins. Continue along this path for a little over two miles to Blackness Castle.

Blackness Castle stands on a rocky promontory like a sentinel. Facing seaward and projecting into the Forth it represents the hull of a ship. There has probably been a harbour and some form of defensive building on this spot since Roman times. Some local historians have even said that this is the site of Ceir Eden (the end of the Antonine Wall).

The castle which can be seen today was built in stages between the fifteenth and sixteenth centuries. Its predecessor, belonging to the Douglas family, was destroyed by fire in 1443 during their dispute with James II over the crown of Scotland.

It seems that the castle has remained in ruins for some time, though in 1465 the burgesses of Linlithgow were granted a charter to build a new port using the stones from the burnt-out castle. Shortly after this new port was constructed the English fleet attacked and burned the ships lying within its shelter. The Hamilton family had the castle rebuilt in its present form and from time to time it has been used as a prison. In fact, at one time it was Scotland's chief state prison. Throughout the ages its unfortunate inmates included Cardinal Beaton (1543), the Earl of Angus (1544), and a number of Covenantors were held there in 1660.

From the time of the Napoleonic Wars until the early part of this century, the castle was used as an arsenal. Today, the castle is undergoing a large programme of restoration by Historic Buildings Scotland.

The way continues along the shore past Carriden House and the many Roman remains contained within this area. In fact, the house, which was built in the seventeenth century by Sir John Hamilton of Letterick, stands directly on a Roman fort.

In 1868 a legionary tablet was discovered at Bridgeness at the eastern end of Bo'ness on the site of the Antonine Wall and is marked by a plaque in Harbour Road. (This is described in the chapter four, The Union Canal.)

The path ends at the outskirts of Bo'ness and the way continues through the streets into the town.

Borrowstounness takes its name from Borrowstoun (a hamlet situated on the Old Linlithgow Road) and 'ness' refers to its coastal location. Historically a centre for a wide variety of industries, including brewing, carting, mining, distilling, flax dressing, fishing, shipbuilding, silk-making, soap-making and whaling, Bo'ness has suffered a great deal through their decline.

Bo'ness has been a port since the middle of the sixteenth century. It was established by the Duchess of Hamilton and her husband, the Earl of Selkirk. By the middle of the eighteenth century it was considered to be Scotland's third largest port. The first harbour dates from 1707 and the one which you can see today dates from 1881.

Bo'ness was almost the proud possessor of its own canal. When it was decided to build the Forth and Clyde Canal, the burghers of Bo'ness vociferously opposed its beginning in Grangemouth. They felt that since Bo'ness had superior harbour facilities it would be considerably better suited to being used as the canal's eastern sea lock. So when the canal was finally built at Grangemouth, the determined burghers decided to build a link from Lock Two to Bo'ness harbour. They also set up their own Borrowstounness Canal Company. This company successfully steered two Acts through Parliament, raised £10,000 and set about building their canal. From the River Avon a canal running eastward to within a mile of the town was cut and an aqueduct across the Avon was nearly completed when the work was abandoned through lack of funds.

Some years later the Canal Company tried to resume the project, however, Robert Whitworth, the engineer who completed the Forth and Clyde Canal, estimated that the cost would be £17,763. This sum was too much for the company and reluctantly they abandoned the scheme once again. This was to prove catastrophic to the prosperity of the port whose revenue fell by a factor of 10 within five years, thanks to its rival at Grangemouth.

Coal mining has, until recently, been the mainstay of Bo'ness' industry with the large Kinneil Colliery the main employer in the area. However, this colliery, one of the biggest in Scotland, closed in 1984. Opened in the 1950s, it was one of the early super-pits which worked directly with Valleyfield Colliery near Culross on the opposite bank of the Forth to extract the coal from the rich seams under the river. These seams have been tapped for many hundreds of years, beginning in the thirteen century when the monks of Hollyrood were granted a title to a colliery at Carriden. Many of the local landowners, including the powerful Hamilton family, owned pits and at the end of the nineteenth century there was almost one hundred independent pits being worked in the area.

In the town itself, many of the interesting old buildings have been renovated, preserving their original character. These include Bo'ness library in Scotland's Close, which was a former eighteenth-century tavern; the eighteenth-century tobacco warehouse, which is now converted into flats, also in Scotland's Close; and the nineteenth-century granary in North Street.

Perhaps the most exciting feature about Bo'ness is the Bo'ness and Kinneil Steam Railway. From its humble beginnings in 1979, the Scottish Railway Preservation Society has transformed this site beside the old dock basin into the embodiment of a working steam railway. A Victorian station was brought lock, stock and barrel from Wormit in Fife, and rebuilt on this site. An engine shed dating from 1842 from Haymarket Station in Edinburgh and Hamilton's Cottage, a workers' cottage depicting life in the 1920s has also been preserved. Throughout the summer, SRPS run a regular service via Kinneil Halt to Birkhill Station – a distance of almost five miles.

From there it is but a short walk to the beautiful Avon Gorge where Birkhill Fire Clay Mine sits in the hillside. The mine contains 300-million-year-old fossils in the walls and ceiling. There is also an audio-visual presentation which shows exactly what it was like to work in a mine in the past. For those who enjoy a look at the area's industrial heritage, or even those who don't, a trip on the railway and a look down the mine is a great day out.

From Kinneil Halt it is only a short walk to Kinneil House, the ancient seat of the Hamilton family. Originally, the building would have been a feudal keep and probably dates from the reign of David I in the twelfth century. During the turbulent years just after the reign of Mary Queen of Scots the house was pillaged once and burned down twice between 1559 and 1570 as Protestants and Catholics fought for control of the country. The building which is seen today is an amalgam of the early keep, the sixteenth-century mansion and the north and south wings which were built by the Duchess Anne in the seventeenth century to join the two previous structures together. The building is in a remarkable state of preservation having been re-roofed and re-floored during this century.

Within the grounds there is also much to see. Directly behind the house there are the remains of a workshop which was used by James Watt in the early development of the steam engine. Watt came to Kinneil in 1769, entering into partnership with Doctor John Roebuck who at that time resided at Kinneil House. Roebuck was developing the coal pits around Bo'ness for the supply of fuel to the Carron Iron Works. Earlier, he had installed a Newcommen steam engine to deal with the problem of flooding within the pits but this engine was found to be inadequate for the job. Hearing of Watt's experiments to improve steam engines, Roebuck solicited his help. However, the experiments carried out at Kinneil were largely unsuccessful.

A few hundred metres to the west of Kinneil House is the site of the ancient village of Kinneil. This village predates Bo'ness and was probably founded in the eleventh century.

Kinneil was built close to the site of the Roman fortlet which formed part of the Antonine Wall. The ruins of the church gable are all that remains of the village today. There is an ancient legend which says that St Serf stood on this site in the sixth century and threw his staff across the Forth. The staff came to rest and blossomed at Culross and so the saint founded the abbey there.

The way now continues to Linlithgow. Walk to the end of Harbour Road and then turn left into Grahamsdyke Road. Then take the first on the right into Drum Road at the end of which a footpath continues to Borrowstoun Road. Here turn right and follow this road to its end. Then turn left into Linlithgow Road and take the second right into Crawfield Road. Some 300m along this road a footpath begins.

Follow this to where it joins a minor road. Turn right and then take the first left on to another footpath which comes out on the B8029 or Mill Road just north of Linlithgow. Follow this road south to Listloaning Road at the end of which there is a footpath which joins Main Street Linlithgow. Walk east along Main Street, which becomes Falkirk Road, then along West Port and High Street. Turn right into Preston Road and there you will find the Union Canal once again.

Preston Road also provides access to Beecraigs Country Park as well as to the many historical sites within the Bathgate Hills, such as Torphican Abbey, Cairnpapple, Carribar Castle and the Earth Fort of Peaceknowe to name but a few.

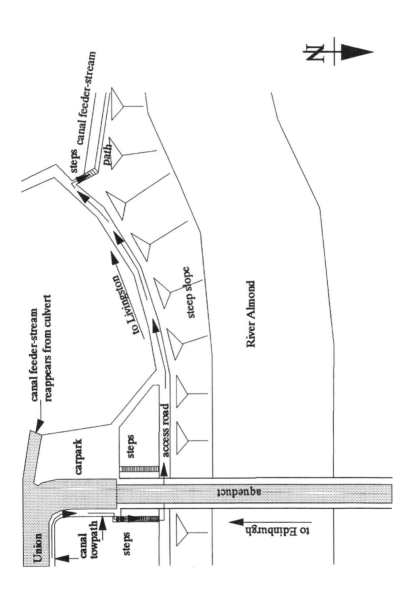

CHAPTER SIX

The Union Canal to Dalkeith over the Pentland Hills

Since some people may wish to miss out the two city stretches of the Central Scottish Way, this chapter outlines an alternative to the route through Edinburgh, just as chapter one provided an alternative walk around Glasgow. I would point out, however, that the following route, although perhaps more rural in setting has, by necessity, to use much more of the public road system than the route which goes through the capital.

After the traveller has crossed the aqueduct which spans the River Almond a set of steps can be seen at the south-east corner. Go down these 42 steps to the road below; turn left under the aqueduct and follow this access road for about 450m. On the right is another set of steps leading down to a lower level. Follow them to the bottom where a pathway which follows the line of the canal's feeder-stream begins. This path continues, through a pleasant wooded aspect, for two-and-a-half miles until it joins Almondell Country Park.

This delightful estate was once owned by Henry Erskine, who was reckoned to be one of the most brilliant members of the Scottish Bar in the latter part of the eighteenth century. He built the mansion house, planted trees, many of which are still in existence today, and constructed a bridge over the Almond in 1800. The house was so badly built that Erskine's son, who

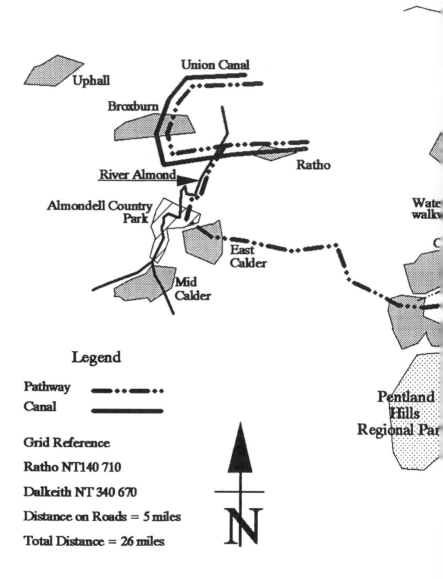

Uphall

Union Canal

Broxburn

Ratho

River Almond

Almondell Country
Park

East
Calder

Mid
Calder

Wate
walkw

Pentland
Hills
Regional Par

Legend

Pathway

Canal

Grid Reference

Ratho NT140 710

Dalkeith NT 340 670

Distance on Roads = 5 miles

Total Distance = 26 miles

N

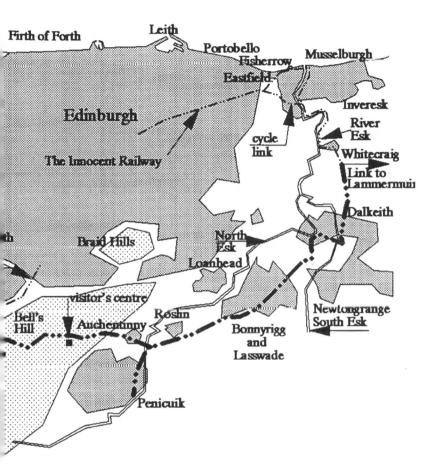

Firth of Forth

Leith

Portobello
Fisherrow

Musselburgh

Eastfield

Inveresk

Edinburgh

cycle
link

River
Esk

The Innocent Railway

Whitecraig

Link to
Lammermuir

Dalkeith

Braid Hills

North
Esk

th

Loanhead

visitor's centre

Roslin

Newtongrange
South Esk

Bell's
Hill

Auchendinny

Bonnyrigg
and
Lasswade

Penicuik

took on the family title of Earl of Buchan from his uncle, had to have it extensively refurbished. However, he seldom spent any time there. The house fell into disrepair and had to be demolished by the army in 1969. The Naysmith bridge was also neglected and in 1970 it collapsed. The Nelson Mandela Bridge was built to replace this crossing.

Cross this bridge and take the path past the visitors' centre, once the estate's stables, where there is a Natural History exhibition and a tea-room. Travel on past the Dell Bridge, which was built to take the main estate drive over the Dell Burn. Here you will find a stone with the inscription 'M.S. Gul. Vallas Octob: XV. MDCCLXXXIV'. It means: 'Sacred to the memory of William Wallace, 15 October 1784' and it was erected by the eleventh Earl of Buchan who was a great patriot and admirer of Sir William Wallace. He also had a statue of Scotland's Champion erected at Bemersyde near Dryburgh (described in chapter nine). His wife, Margaret, Countess of Buchan, being of kindred spirit, erected a similar stone in another part of the estate, in memory of her ancestor, Sir Simon Fraser, who was a staunch supporter of King Robert the Bruce and the dates on both stones are the same.

Cross the river at the little aqueduct which carries the canal feeder-stream to the opposite bank and climb up the steep path on the right to the top of the adjacent Camps Viaduct.

Camps Viaduct, the railway viaduct, was built by the North British Railway Company in 1885 to service the mines, limeworks and oil works of Pumpherston and Uphall. This line was closed in 1956 but could soon carry the Edinburgh to Glasgow Cycleway across the River Almond.

Once the traveller has joined the railway solum turn left and within half a mile this track comes out at Main Street, East Calder.

Cross this road and join the track on the other side which will take you out of the village in a south-easterly direction. After a short distance this track will join a minor road. Turn left here and follow this road (via the A71 for 50m or so) to where it joins the B7031 to Kirknewton. Turn right at this

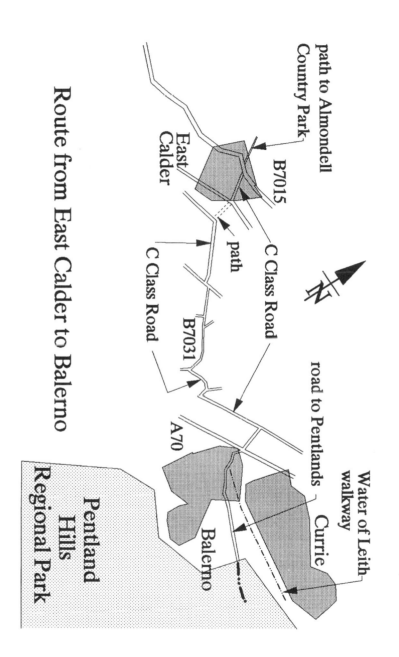

Route from East Calder to Balerno

path to Almondell Country Park

B7015

East Calder

C Class Road

path

C Class Road

B7031

A70

N

road to Pentlands

Water of Leith walkway

Currie

Balerno

Pentland Hills Regional Park

Camp's Viaduct in Almondell Park

junction and follow the minor road signed for Currie. After about four miles on this road, passing Dalmahoy Country Club on the left, there is another minor road to the right signposted for Balerno. Take this road into Balerno and then carry on to Malleny Mills. Once here, follow the path between Harbour Hill and Bell's Hill going past Glencorse Reservoir down through Flotterstone Glen to the Information Centre. Just beyond this is Flotterstone Inn.

Pass the inn and turn right on to the main Edinburgh to Biggar road, the A702, and carry along this road for half a mile. Then turn left and carry on all the way to Belwood Road. Continue down this road to the junction with the Edinburgh Road, the A701. Cross this into Grahams Road now in Auchendinny. Continue down this road, going past a junction to reach a path which leads directly to the Penicuik to Dalkeith cycle path. Turn left on this path and walk in the direction of Dalkeith. The route follows the solum of the now disused Edinburgh to Peebles Railway which was closed in 1969.

Shortly after joining the walkway, you will arrive at a railway tunnel. Although it is not particularly long, it might be a good idea to bring a torch on darker days.

Continuing to Dalkeith, the route passes across the Firth Viaduct which offers a good view of the surrounding countryside, including the Pentland Hills.

Travel on to the point where a minor road passes over the cycle track. By turning right on to this road the traveller can gain access to the Roslin Glen Country Park. The way continues along the cycle track past Roslin Castle Station, the sign of which is printed in seashells.

The route continues on to Rosewell, a small mining village with its uniform rows of miners' cottages. This village has little historical value except as possibly the best example in Scotland of a company village. However, within a mile radius of Rosewell many places of great significance are located, including the village of Roslin with its Collegiate Chapel which was built in 1446 by the third Earl of Orkney and which is famous for its apprentice pillar and beautifully ornate ceiling; Hawthornden Castle with its prehistoric man-made caves below the castle which, in 1338, were used by Alexander Ramsay and his men as a retreat between campaigns to free Scottish castles from the hands of the English; and Woodhouselee Castle which was built for the Purves family in 1664.

The route continues on for a further two miles to pass through southern Lasswade and Bonnyrigg. Collectively this is a comparatively modern place which grew from the area's industrial base of coal mining and paper milling, although

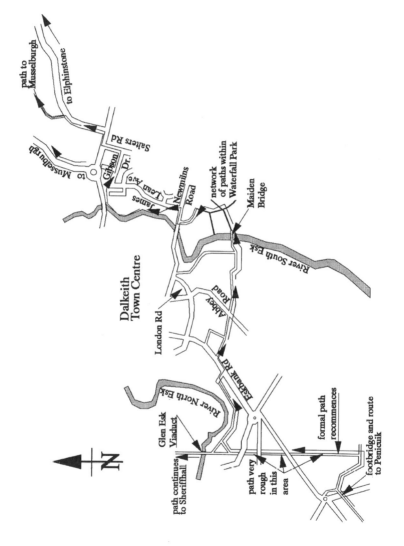

the original small village of Lasswade has existed for a much longer time.

One-and-a-half miles to the south, along the road to Gorebridge, is situated Dalhousie Castle. This is the ancient seat of the noble Norman Ramsay family. This castle, now a hotel, has been drastically altered throughout the centuries, although it still contains its ancient core with its drawbridge and gatehouse.

A mile after passing Lasswade and Bonnyrigg the formal cycle route ends. Continue over a footbridge and then turn right and go down a rough road for 200m or so to where the path continues on the left. At this point the traveller may take a short detour to Lady Victoria Colliery in Newtongrange which is now the Scottish Mining Museum. Travel along the disused railway line in a southerly direction, to Newtongrange behind the colliery.

Staying with the route to Dalkeith, take the path which heads in a northerly direction even though, at the time of writing, it has not been upgraded to a formal cycle track and is rather muddy and overgrown in some places.

Within a mile this track joins the footpath along the banks of the River North Esk, almost reaching Glen Esk Viaduct before doubling back in a southerly direction. Glen Esk Viaduct was constructed in 1847 by the North British Railway Company and was restored in 1992 by Midlothian District Council on behalf of Edinburgh Greenbelt Trust.

The traveller is now within the picturesque and historical burgh town of Dalkeith which was, up until local government reorganisation in 1975, the county town of Midlothian and owing to the recent reorganisation holds this title again.

Dalkeith, like most of the other sizable towns in the area, has a long and eventful history starting in feudal times. The name Dalkeith is most probably of Celtic origin and means 'the entrance to a narrow dale'. It was mentioned in a charter granted by David I gifting 52 acres of land to the monks of Holyrood Abbey in 1128. This charter was witnessed by William de Graham, the feudal lord in the area.

The Norman family of De Graham seem to have been in Scotland possibly from the time of Malcolm II and by David I's rule were a well-established feudal family. The family built Dalkeith Castle, one of the oldest residences in Midlothian. They resided there until the middle of the fourteenth century when Marjory Graham married William Douglas of Lugton and the Castle of Dalkeith passed into the hands of the house of Douglas who retained their possession for 300 years. In 1406 Sir James Douglas founded the church of St Nicholas, one of the earliest collegiate churches in Scotland, which has now been incorporated into Dalkeith Parish Church. When the plague reached Edinburgh in 1519 the Earl of Arran removed King James V to Dalkeith Castle where the court was held for a month.

The castle was bought by Walter Scott, Earl of Buccleuch, in 1642. The earl had two daughters, Mary and Anne. After her father's death in 1651, Mary became Countess of Buccleuch and was married at the age of 11. She died at the age of 14 and was succeeded by her younger sister, Anne, who in turn was married when she was 12 to Charles II's son, the Duke of Monmouth. The couple became the Duke and Duchess of Monmouth, Duke and Duchess of Buccleuch and Count and Countess of Dalkeith and the castle at Dalkeith became the Palace of Dalkeith. Later the duke was to fall foul of his uncle, James II or VII, and was executed.

Today the palace (or Dalkeith House as it's now known) and grounds are open to the public in the summer. The grounds are now a country park and contain a deer forest which is thought to be the only part of the ancient Caledonian Forest still in existence in southern Scotland.

The route through the town is as follows. The path along the riverside ends at Cemetery Road. Turn right here and then take the first left on to Eskbank Road. Cross this road, going past St David's Church and then turn right on to the footpath which passes the bowling green and tennis courts and which continues on to Abbey Road. Cross Abbey Road and continue east along the path, past Dalkeith Golf Club carpark and club house, through Benbright Wood and on to cross Maiden Bridge.

This bridge, which is thought to be of Roman construction, got its name because the young maiden princess, Margaret, eldest daughter of Henry VII of England who was betrothed to King James IV of Scotland, passed across it on her way to meet the Scottish nobles and the Archbishop of Glasgow at Newbattle Abbey. Here the marriage contract was signed and the noble Lords of Scotland accepted the young princess into their custody and escorted her to Edinburgh for the royal wedding. This marriage bound together the blood lines of the royal families of Scotland and England and resulted in the Union of the Crowns.

Newbattle Abbey is a little over a quarter of a mile further south. The Cistercian monks first came to this area in 1140 from Melrose, 'the aldbotyl or old house', to Newbattle the *newbotyl* or 'new house'. This district is now known once again by its ancient name of Monklands.

The monks were traditionally farmers who, as legend will have it, discovered coal while tending their sheep. They opened mines in many parts of the Lothians and beyond. Indeed, at the height of modern coal mining in Central Scotland most of the collieries were in areas which the Newbattle monks had first mined.

During the history of Newbattle Abbey it has been burned down twice, once by Richard II in 1387 and the second time by the Earl of Hertford in 1544. It was never again rebuilt. Much of the stone went to build Newbattle House on the same site and incorporated into the design of the house are the remnants of the abbey. This part of the house is known as the crypt and it still contains a chapel. Inside the chapel is Mary Queen of Scots' baptismal font which was plundered from Linlithgow.

The last Abbot of Newbattle, Mark Ker, sided with the reformers during the troubles of 1560 and, after the dissolution of the monasteries, held on to the Abbey as a trustee of the estate. His son, also Mark Ker, had the title of Earl of Lothian

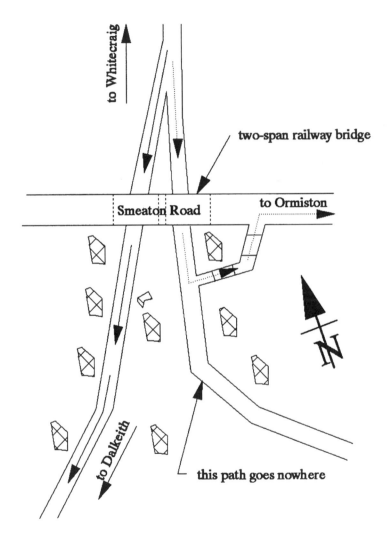

to Whitecraig

two-span railway bridge

Smeaton Road

to Ormiston

to Dalkeith

this path goes nowhere

N

conferred upon him by King James VI in 1604 and it was he who built the house which now exists as a short-course and conference centre.

When the foundations for the residential extension were being dug in the 1960s, a great number of human remains were exhumed. They were later found to be from the twelfth century, making them some of the earliest monks to have lived at the monastery. They were held at the college until 1990 when they were reinterred in the Lothian family cemetery in the grounds of Newbattle Abbey.

Turn left in Waterfall Park and follow the path north to the access road which climbs up to Newmilns Road.

Cross Newmilns Road and continue along James Lean Avenue. A little way along this road, opposite Newmilns Terrace on the left, there is a footpath leading down to the top of the riverbank. Follow this footpath along the top of the steep bank to where it joins a grassy knoll and walk up the slope to join Gibson Drive. From here take the first left into Salters Road and after a few hundred metres turn right and then first left on to the Elphinstone-Tranent Road, the B6414.

Pass the Thornybank Industrial Estate at the edge of Dalkeith. On the left the path goes along a disused railway solum. Join this path and after a little over a half a mile the route comes to a double-arch railway bridge at Smeaton. Turn right at this bridge.

To reach Lauder, head up the stepped ramp to the road running over the bridge and turn right.

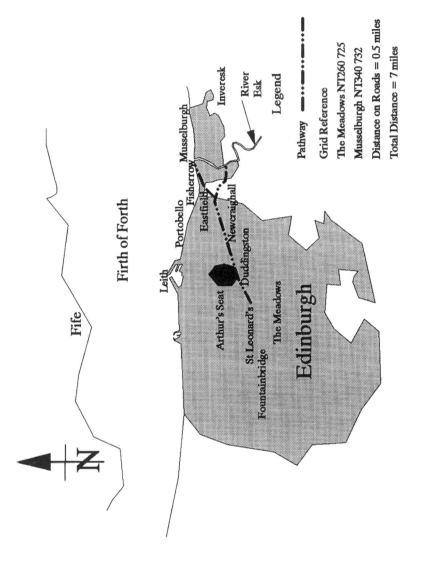

N

Fife

Firth of Forth

Leith

Portobello

Musselburgh

Fisherrow

Inveresk

Eastfield

Newcraighall

Duddingston

Arthur's Seat

St Leonard's

The Meadows

Fountainbridge

Edinburgh

River Esk

Legend

Pathway

Grid Reference

The Meadows NT260 725

Musselburgh NT340 732

Distance on Roads = 0.5 miles

Total Distance = 7 miles

CHAPTER SEVEN

The Innocent Railway

This route not only embraces the Innocent Railway but also includes the Meadows for, within the network of these pathways, together with the Union Canal, it forms the basis for a mainly off-road route through the city from west to east.

The route leaves the Union Canal at Gilmour Park, crosses over the canal by the Leamington Road lifting-bridge and then turns left into Lower Gilmour Place. Go left again into Gilmour Place and then turn right into Leven Street passing the King's Theatre. The King's Theatre, built in 1905, has been the home of Edinburgh's yearly pantomime ever since.

The route then continues from Leven Street. Turn left off Leven Street and head into Valleyfield, go left again into Leven Terrace and on to the Meadows Walkway. Cross Melville Drive by the Toucan Crossing and continue along North Meadow Walk.

The park area known as the Meadows was created in the early part of the eighteenth century by draining the South Loch. This had been the source of water for many of the local distilleries but at the end of the seventeenth century it was so depleted that the Town Council decided to have it drained. One of the park's earliest gardeners was William Burness, the father of Scotland's national poet, Robert Burns.

A few hundred metres further on the junction with Middle

Meadow Walk is located; this route provides access to the city centre. Continue along North Meadow Walk, travelling past the tennis courts and bowling greens to Hope Park Crescent. Turn right at this junction and then quickly left into Hope Park Terrace. This leads on to South Clerk Street. Cross the road and head along Bernard Terrace and into St Leonard's Street.

On the other side of St Leonard's Street is the old building of St Leonard's Station, once the town terminus of the Edinburgh and Dalkeith Railway. The coat of arms of the railway company still hangs above the door of this now refurbished house. Opposite is Parkside Street where there is a carpark (once a railway marshalling yard). The route

Old St Leonard's Station

Innocent Railway Tunnel entrance

continues through the carpark into a new housing estate with
nameless streets.

After leaving the carpark, simply turn left, then first right,
then again first left and walk down a short hill to East Parkside
where the Innocent Railway Cycle Route is signposted. Just
off East Parkside, tucked into the left alongside a block of flats,
is the entrance to the tunnel of the Edinburgh and Dalkeith
Railway (the Innocent Railway).

The Innocent Railway Cycleway starts a little nearer the
Old Town in Viewcraig Gardens before joining East Parkside.

The 518m-long former Edinburgh and Dalkeith Railway
tunnel is one of the oldest railways built in Scotland and is

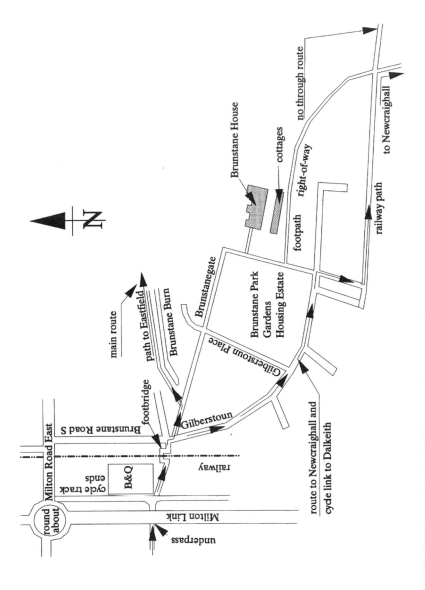

the oldest one to carry passengers. It was planned and built between 1826 and 1831 by Edinburgh engineer James Jardine at a cost of £80,000, the biggest single expenditure being the tunnel which had to be driven under part of Arthur's Seat and ran all the way to Newton.

The railway was driven by horse power and it was the first one to be built in Scotland. Its name, the Innocent Railway, was first applied by Doctor James Chalmers, who spoke of its simplicity – there was no need for intermediate stations as passengers were able to join or alight at will along its length. Later, this name was to signify its unique record in being completely accident free.

Steam *was* used in the tunnel under Arthur's Seat where, because of the steep gradient of 1 in 30, horse power was not adequate. As soon as enough waggons were collected, the same number at the top and the bottom of the tunnel, they were coupled together and attached to a five-inch-thick cable driven by two 25-horsepower steam engines. The descending waggons were balanced by the ascending ones. Once at the other side of the tunnel the waggons were uncoupled and once more continued their journey by horse power.

For the first three years the railway was used exclusively for the movement of coal from the nearby Midlothian pits, but the novelty of the railway soon led to its popularity as a passenger carrier. In the years that followed, this railway provided thousands of people with a cheap link to and from the city of Edinburgh and in the first four years of operation it carried over a million passengers.

There are many stories written about the early days of this railway. One tells of a farmer's wife who announced that she had lost her shopping basket. The driver at once stopped, unhitched his horse and sent his assistant cantering back along the line to search the tunnel for it. After the truck had been stopped for about 40 minutes, the woman remembered she had left her bag at home.

The railway was extended several times with a branch line opening in 1834 to Fisherrow in Musselburgh, and in 1838 the

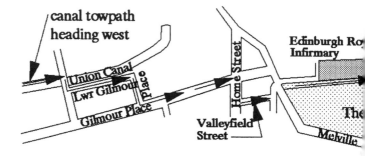

Central Link

main line was extended to Dalkeith together with a further branch to Leith.

Today the route through the tunnel may seem like a daunting task, but I have never encountered anything which gave me any cause for concern, indeed, the well-lit tunnel is kept clean, free of litter and broken glass.

After emerging on the other side of the tunnel the way continues past Arthur's Seat, an extinct volcano. Towering high above are the rock faces of Lion's Haunch and Samson's Ribs. Between Arthur's Seat and the cycle route are the Bonnie Wells o' Wearie, which were immortalised in the song of the same name, situated close to Duddingston Loch. It was here

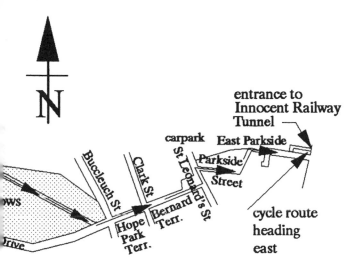

on 18 September 1745 that Charles Edward Stewart had his troops breach the wall and march into the King's Park.

The Young Pretender, accompanied by many of his faithful noblemen, then rode on to St Antonies Wall from where he was able to survey for the first time the palace of his ancestors, Holyrood House. Later that day he entered the palace amidst a vast crowd of spectators loudly expressing their joy at this event. The Prince stayed in the palace for only two days, preferring to stay close to his troops who were camped at Duddingston. The next day he led his troops to meet the opposing royal army under Lieutenant-General Sir John Cope who were now marching towards Edinburgh. The two

131

Fisherrow Harbour

armies met at Prestonpans where the Prince and his army of Highlanders celebrated another resounding victory.

The area adjacent to the cycleway is part of the Duddingston Nature Reserve which supports large number of many species of wildfowl. To the south is Prestonfield Golf Club; its championship course was once the venue for many prestigious golf tournaments. This stretch of the cycleway ends at Duddingston Road West. The ancient Duddingston Village is only a few hundred metres to the left and Craigmillar Castle is about a kilometre to the right.

The name Duddingston seems to have derived from the Saxon family name 'Dodin' – *Dodinstun* meaning 'the land belonging to Dodin'. This Saxon family were obviously very powerful because there is considerable evidence that they were signatories of various charters up to the reign of Malcolm IV. Therefore, they belong to a small minority of noble Saxon families in Scotland, who managed to hold on to their lands through the reign of David I when most of the land in Scotland was handed over to Norman overlords and the feudal system was introduced.

A church was built by the monks of Kelso on the shore of Duddingston Loch in 1143 and some of this original structure still survives today as part of Duddingston Parish Church.

Duddingston still maintains its picturesque village character, with its main street, the Causeway, running past the old village inn, the Sheep's Heid, which was said to have been frequented by James VI.

The ancient Craigmillar Castle, although too far off the route of the Innocent Railway to describe here, is still very much worth a visit.

After crossing Duddingston Road West the clearly defined cycle path carries on uninterrupted to Duddingston Park South.

Cross the park and follow the path through an underpass over which runs the Musselburgh Bypass. The cycleway turns left here and within a very short distance comes to an end at Milton Road East.

From the east side of the underpass there are two routes, the first is as follows: follow the signs for Brunstane and take the footbridge over the railway to Gilberstoun. The first route starts where the traveller comes to a sign on the left, for Eastfield, at Daiches Braes. Here there is a ramp which leads down to a walkway alongside the Brunstane Burn. This new walkway ends at the junction of Musselburgh Road and Milton Road East, in Joppa.

To return to Edinburgh, cross this main road and travel to the end of Eastfield Place and join the Portobello Promenade.

Going in the opposite direction along Musselburgh Road, however, you will shortly arrive at Fisherrow Harbour where Musselburgh Promenade provides a link to the south and east. The second route starts once more at Gilberstoun.

It is interesting to note that the name of this street has been misspelt. It should read 'Gilbertoun', which was the fourteenth-century name for Brunstane House which is located close by. This house, which is now split into two residences, has had a long and sometimes turbulent history and the following references are taken from a pamphlet written by resident Sean Higgnet.

In 1545 the estate descended to Alexander Crighton. Crighton, who was ready to swear allegiance to any cause likely to line his pockets, joined forces with the Duke of Somerset whose army was passing through the lands of Brunstane on its way to sack Leith and Edinburgh. As a result of this act of treachery the Scottish Privy Council ordered the destruction of the houses of Saltoun, Ormiston and Gilbertoun.

In the event, only the roof of Brunstane was removed in a half-hearted attempt to make the house uninhabitable. Crighton Castle, however, some ten miles inland, was almost completely destroyed.

When the Duke of Somerset returned to Scotland in 1547 Crighton switched his allegiance to the Scottish cause and allowed the Scottish army, who were awaiting the invaders, to camp in the fields around Brunstane. The opposing armies met at Pinkie, a few miles to the east, and the Scots were heavily defeated. The remnants of the Scottish army fled back through Brunstane, 'place of the Lords of Brimston', where, according to the English General Patton, 'the dead bodies lay as thik as a man may note cattel grazing.'

Patton's spelling, incidentally, makes plain the meaning of Brunstane which is the old Scots for 'brimstone' or sulphur, a substance that still carries with it associations of witchcraft and sorcery.

John Crighton, son of Alexander Crighton, again changed sides to support the English. This angered the Auld Alliance of French and Scottish forces and in November 1558 the French garrison stationed at Leith marched forth with the intention of burning and destroying 'the Laird of Brunstane's place'. The French were met by Crighton and the English army at Restalrig and were repulsed, so Brunstane survived again.

In 1592 the Crighton's numerous estates were sold off and today Brunstane House consists of two private residences which are only open to the public on 'Open Doors Day', which is normally in mid September.

The route from Gilberstoun is important as the link to the River Esk walkway some three miles to the north-east. Turn right at the railway footbridge and follow Gilberstoun into a new housing estate called Brunstane Park Gardens. Take the fourth turning on the right on to a wide footpath which links the housing estate to a dismantled railway. Follow this railway solum for about a quarter of a mile to where a small footpath goes off to the right. This footpath joins Newcraighall Road, or Whitehill Street, within the village of Newcraighall itself.

The village of Newcraighall was until recently a mining village. It was founded by Sir Archibald Hope in 1827 when he built a row of traditional but and ben cottages and named them New Craighall.

In addition to the pits at Wanton Walls and Niddrie, the Klondyke pit was opened at Newcraighall in 1897. This huge pit, with many of its mine roads going far under the estuary of the Forth, employed 1,000 miners who produced 250,000 tons of coal a year. It was closed in 1968 and in 1971 Edinburgh Corporation recommended that the village should be demolished and issued notices to all its residents.

However, the villagers fought to save it and one year later the village of Newcraighall was reprieved and subsequently rebuilt, retaining its original character. The only building left in the village reminiscent of its mining days is the Miners Welfare Institute.

Continue along Whitehill Street in a westerly direction, past the now refurbished but and ben miners' cottages with their beautiful gardens, and on to the pedestrian crossing. Cross here and continue in the same direction to Newcraighall Drive. Go along this to Park View where, at a white triangular gate, the cycleway starts again in Newcraighall Park. Follow the tree-lined avenue adjacent to the railway as it turns to run parallel along the A1 at the top of the slope. On leaving the park, the cycle track continues to run adjacent to the road.

After about 300m there is a bridge under the A1 which is signposted for Niddrie via Whitehill Road. Pass this marker, continuing in the same direction until the junction of Mucklets Road. This road finishes at Musselburgh Station and is now restricted to walkers and cyclists only. It is a good place to take a train either back to Edinburgh or on to a station further south or east.

At Musselburgh Station turn right and follow the sign for the Esk Walkway. This path follows the railway to Wanton Walls junction at which the path goes under the railway. Turn left on the other side of the railway bridge and head for the River Esk. Turn right to reach Monkton Hall.

Our route goes left, so follow the railway once again to reach another bridge about 100m further on. Go under this and into a housing estate.

Follow the cycle route through this small estate and on to Monktonhall Terrace. Then follow the sign for Whitecraig which means crossing Monktonhall Terrace and continuing on into Ferguson Drive. At the end of Ferguson Drive a small road, bounded by Monktonhall Golf Course, leads to within a quarter of a mile of a footbridge, across which is the River Esk walkway.

Turn left for Musselburgh and right for Haddington.

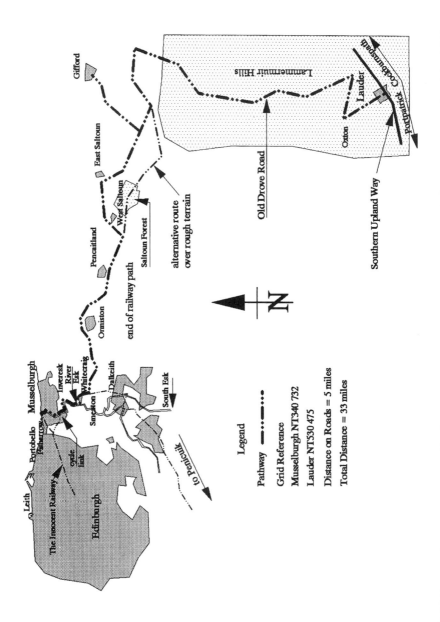

Leith

Portobello

Musselburgh

Fisherrow

cycle link

The Innocent Railway

Edinburgh

Inveresk

River Esk

Whitecraig

Smeaton

Dalkeith

South Esk

to Penicuik

Ormiston

Pencaitland

end of railway path

Saltoun Forest

West Saltoun

alternative route over rough terrain

East Saltoun

Gifford

N

Lammermuir Hills

Old Drove Road

Oxton

Lauder

Cockburnspath

Portpatrick

Southern Upland Way

Legend

Pathway

Grid Reference

Musselburgh NT340 732

Lauder NT530 475

Distance on Roads = 5 miles

Total Distance = 33 miles

CHAPTER EIGHT

Fisherrow to Lauder

Musselburgh was a port of some importance at the time of the brief occupation of southern Scotland by the Romans. It was they who built the first harbour on the spot where Fisherrow Harbour now exists. As its name suggests, the early settlement known as Eskmuthe (Musselburgh) was situated around this harbour and the mouth of the river.

Nearby Inveresk Hill, long associated with Celtic ceremonies, and the site chosen for the Roman temple to Apollo, has retained its religious significance in Christian times. The earliest record of a church on the hill comes from the beginning of the eleventh century and this church was known as Muscilburg.

The first charter in the area was granted by Malcolm IV in 1193 who gifted the lands around Musselburgh and Inveresk to the monks of Dunfermline Abbey. The monks held them until the Reformation when they were transferred to the bailies of the Town Council. It was on these lands of Great and Little Inveresk that the Lords of Scotland swore allegiance to William the Lion in 1165.

Musselburgh is known as the Honest Toun. The origin of this name is said to derive from the time, just after Robert the Bruce's death, when Scotland was being governed by its Regent, Thomas Randolph, who had been created Earl

The planned village of Gifford

of Moray in 1312. While leading an army south against the English who were preparing to invade Scotland Randolph was taken ill at Wallyford. The troops were sent on and Randolph was taken to Musselburgh, to the old inn at Pinkie Gate, where the burghers of the town took it in turn to guard him night and day until his death in July 1332.

When Donald Earl of Mar, nephew of King Robert, took

140

over as Regent and wished to reward the burghers for their devotion they declined, saying that it had been but their solemn duty to protect the most precious life in the country. Mar is then said to have remarked, 'Sure you are a set of honest fellows.' From that time the town has proudly borne the motto *Honestas*.

The area around Musselburgh has been the site of some famous battles, including the Battle of Pinkie in September 1547. This terrible defeat was inflicted on the Scots by Henry VIII's army during the Rough Wooing. Thousands of Scots were killed. So great was the slaughter that it was said that the Almond was choked with bodies and the Pinkie Burn ran with blood for three solid days and nights. According to English records of the time, a further 1,500 Scots were taken prisoner. The rest of this vanquished army were chased to the gates of Edinburgh.

During the Battle of Carberry in June 1567 not a shot was fired or any blow struck. The sum and substance of this encounter between Mary Queen of Scots and the Earl of Bothwell, and the Confederate Lords, was that for many hours, between many threats, the lords urged their queen to rid herself of her third husband. Eventually, Bothwell was given safe conduct out of the country and he spent the rest of his life in exile in Denmark.

Many of the town's buildings are in the Georgian style but some pre-date that period. Two of note are the tolbooth, first built in 1496 then refurbished and extended in 1833, and Pinkie House, which was built in the sixteenth century. The latter is now part of the famous Loretto School.

The town also has an association with Sir Walter Scott. On a plaque outside the tolbooth an inscription states: 'Sir Walter Scott, created Honorary Burgess of Musselburgh 25 March 1799, resided in the Honest Toun periodically from 1797 to 1808 while on duty as quartermaster of the Edinburgh Light Horse and there wrote many stanzas of the Lay of the Last Minstrel and of Marmion.'

Throughout the centuries Musselburgh and the

surrounding area have been temporary home to countless numbers of troops. This has built up a long tradition with sport, particularly of the military variety such as archery and horse-racing, although the town, as with most in this area, also has a long association with the game of golf.

Each year on the famous links golf course, where the Open Championship has been played six times, the Royal Company of Archers shoot for the Musselburgh Silver Arrow. The racecourse which now bounds the golf course is one of only three still in existence in Scotland, the others being in Ayr and Kelso, which supply the punter with a full horse-racing card throughout the year.

There has been a tradition in Musselburgh and its environs of Riding the Marches. Possibly originating in feudal times when David II confirmed the ancient rights as a burgh every 21 years, the ceremony marks and reclaims the boundaries of the ancient burgh. Although today Musselburgh is physically joined to its much larger neighbour Edinburgh, it jealously

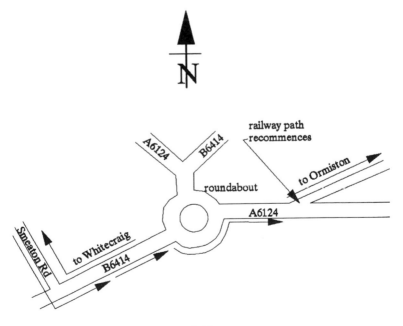

guards its independence and carries out this ancient ceremony with renewed vigour.

The route starts at Fisherrow Harbour and follows the promenade, passing Loretto playing fields, to the River Esk where it crosses the river by Goosegreen Footbridge. Once across the bridge, turn right into Eskside East and follow the river, passing under the bridge at Bridge Street, and continue along the eastern bank to reach the old bridge. This bridge, which was built in medieval times, stands on the same site as the bridge built by the Romans. It was, for hundreds of years, the only place to cross the river Esk for many miles around. Perhaps this is the reason that there were so many conflicts throughout the area's long history.

From here the route crosses Mall Avenue into Station Road, to where the River Esk walkway begins to follow the riverbank.

Follow the walkway for a little less than a mile travelling past the site of a Roman fort and Monktonhall Golf Course, situated on the other side of the river, to arrive at a footbridge which carries the cycleway to Edinburgh. This is where the route described in chapter seven ended and also the place where cyclists going to Musselburgh or Dalkeith will join the route.

Continue along this walkway for just over a mile, ending at the point where it passes under the A1. Then follow the minor road north to the A6094 at Whitecraig.

Turn left and follow the A6094 for the short distance to the end of the village, walking past the BP Service Station and the Dolphin Inn, and there on the other side of the road the cycle route is signposted for Ormiston 5 miles.

After a little over a half a mile at Smeaton the route comes to a double-arch railway bridge. If you take the route through the right-hand arch and keep to the west path for about one mile, you will reach the B6414 Elphinstone Road at the Thornybank Industrial Estate on the edge of Dalkeith. This provides a link with the route described in chapter six.

In the interest of safety, particularly in the second half of this journey, I recommend you take the Ordnance Survey Sheets 66, 72 and 73, together with a compass.

The route to Lauder continues up the stepped ramp to the road above the double-arched bridge and turns right. Carry on to the end of this road and turn left on to the B6414. Follow this road for about quarter of a mile to the roundabout junction with the A6124. Here veer to the right, as signposted, and within about 250m the cycle track starts once again on the left.

The cycle route continues for three miles to Ormiston, passing close to Elphinstone Tower, now demolished, which was the ancient seat of the Lords Elphinstone.

The cycleway passes to the north of Ormiston, a pleasant village with a population of around 2,000. The village, situated on the banks of the River Tyne, was designed in 1735 as a model farming village by John Cockburn and its broad, tree-lined main street still reflects Cockburn's architectural vision. About a mile further south stands Ormiston House, built in 1745, which was the seat of the Cockburn family. It was from the much older house (now restored) close by, that in 1545 George Wishart was arrested by the Earl of Bothwell on the instructions of Cardinal Beaton and taken to St Andrews to be burned at the stake.

Continue on for almost another two miles to Pencaitland, another village in the Tyne Valley which has some of the richest and most abundant agricultural land in Scotland. Its name, meaning 'knoll of the narrow valley', seems to perfectly describe its location.

The village church, part of which was built in the thirteenth century on the foundations of an even earlier building, was extended during the sixteenth and seventeenth centuries. On the west side of the church, secured to the wall, is a chain which was part of a set of jougs – an iron collar used to bind miscreants and to expose them to public humiliation.

Just to the north of the village is situated Winton Castle which was built in 1619 on the site of an earlier castle belonging to the same family. This house, which is one of the best examples of Renaissance architecture in the country, was designed by William Wallace, King James VI's master mason whose other work includes George Heriot's School in Edinburgh. The estate was forfeited by George, fifth Earl Winton, when he was captured at Preston in 1716 whilst fighting on the side of the Old Pretender. He was sentenced to death but managed to escape and live out the rest of his life in Rome, dying in 1749. The castle today is the property of Sir David Ogilvy who often opens his splendid home to the public.

Just about a mile past Pencaitland the traveller will come to the Glenkinchie Distillery. This distillery, which was founded in 1824 as the Kinchie Distillery, was named after the burn situated next to it from which the distillery took its water. It manufactures a fine lowland single malt whisky and it opens all year except Christmas and Ne'erday for guided tours with a wee dram at the end.

The cycle route finishes just under a quarter of a mile past the distillery at a minor road half a mile to the south-west of the village of West Saltoun. There are two villages of Saltoun – West and East Saltoun – and they are approximately a mile apart but they belong to the same parish. The parish of Saltoun had the good fortune of escaping the ravages of the plague which spread through East Lothian in 1645.

Approximately a mile to the south of West Saltoun, on the banks of the River Tyne, is Saltoun Hall. This property came into the hands of the Fletcher family in 1643.

Sir Andrew Fletcher (1653–1716) became a member of the Convention of Estates in 1678 during which he voted against the High Commissioner Lord Lauderdale and opposed the Duke of York (later to become King James II). By this act of defiance he was declared an outlaw. After his involvement in the Duke of Monmouth's rebellion against King James, he was forced to go into exile in Spain in 1681, but returned to Scotland during the revolution against James II.

When King William III of Orange accepted the crown all charges against Fletcher were dropped by the state. He became a member of the last Scottish Parliament and vigorously campaigned against the Act of Union. When his efforts failed and the Act was passed in 1707 Fletcher walked out of the House never to return and later sailed for the Continent. He died in London on his way back to Scotland in 1716 and is buried in Saltoun Kirkyard.

At the end of the cycle path there are two routes both turning left and heading for West Saltoun; at this point the traveller should refer to the Ordnance Survey Maps.

Route one starts about a quarter of a mile down the minor road on the right of which is a small sign for Barley Mill. Take this right-of-way, and go through three gates and along the edge of two fields into Saltoun Forest.

The path through the forest ascends a fairly steep slope and after a quarter of a mile comes to a junction with a wide forestry track. On the right there is another smaller track. Take this smaller track to another junction with a larger track and follow the latter for about 300m. Here a small rough track begins the descent, skirting a field, to Gilchriston and on to the B6368. Cross this road and continue along the minor road. Within two-and-a-quarter miles it comes out at Kidlaw.

The second route follows a series of minor roads.

Follow the road to West Saltoun, turn right to East Saltoun, and then turn right to the junction with the B6368. Here an alternative route, which uses the line of a dismantled railway, goes on to Gifford. The village of Gifford was planned and built by the Marquis of Tweeddale in the early part of the eighteenth century to replace the old village of Bothans which was considered by the Marquis to be too close to Yester House, his new palatial residence. This beautiful village has changed little this century, retaining much of its eighteenth- and nineteenth-century character.

Starting at the village, running parallel to High Street, is the mile-long tree-lined avenue to Yester House. The house, which was built by the fourth Marquis of Tweeddale in 1745, was designed first by James Smith and was later substantially modified by Robert Adam. Close to Yester House is the old Collegiate Church of St Baithen, built by the Lords of Yester

Thirlestane Castle

in 1421, which was once the parish church of the village of Bothans. Since the demise of the village, the grounds have been used as a burial place by the Tweeddale family.

Almost a mile further east along the banks of Gifford Water lie the ruins of the old Castle of Yester which was built by Sir Hugo de Gifford on the lands granted to him by William the Lion in 1190. This estate was acquired by the Hay family in 1418 when Sir William Hay married one of four Gifford daughters. The castle contains a vaulted hall situated entirely below ground level. It is much larger than the normal subterranean prison built into most Scottish castles and the reason for its construction is not known. It is known as Goblin Ha' and, according to Scott's poem, *Marmion*, has links with witchcraft.

Turn right along the B6368 for a short distance and take the first minor road on the left. In just over two miles the road arrives at Kidlaw and joins with the route described above. Alternatively, you may reach Gifford by taking the minor road which dissects your path one mile before Kidlaw.

From Kidlaw follow the minor road past Long Newton, Latch, Over Newton, to Longyester. Here turn right and travel past Blinkbonny Wood and on into the Lammermuir Hills.

The route through the Lammermuir Hills follows a right-of-way, going past Crib Law, Windy Law and the Iron Age fort and standing stones at Tollishill. The route then descends into Lauderdale and connects with a minor road for the last two-and-a-half miles to the Carfraemill Hotel on the A697.

From the hotel there is only one possible way to reach Lauder and the Southern Upland Way, without using either the busy A68 or A697 – follow the unclassified road to Oxton and then continue by the dismantled Lauder branch line of the Waverly Route which closed in 1958.

At Oxton there is a crossroads. Turn left here and follow this minor road for about 400m and there, on the left, is an access to the dismantled railway. From here it is a little under four miles to the Edinburgh Road at the northern end of Lauder. Make sure you have on a stout pair of boots for parts of this railway path can be very muddy.

Lauder is a small but important town. In a charter from King James IV in 1502 it was granted the status of a royal burgh which it held until local government reorganisation in the 1970s. It was, in fact, the only royal burgh in the County of Berwickshire.

To the north-east of the town is situated Thirlestane Castle. This is the family seat of the Maitland-Carews, descendants of the fifteenth Earl of Lauderdale. The lands of Lauderdale were granted to the de Morville family by King David I in the twelfth century and the first keep would date back to this time. King Edward I built a fort here and the English ruled this area for some time before it was taken back for Scotland in 1311.

The present castle was started by John Maitland, Duke of Lauderdale, in the 1590s and two further wings were added in the late seventeenth century. Prince Charles Edward Stuart is thought to have stayed here on his way to England, following the Battle of Prestonpans, and the room in which he was alleged to have stayed is on display.

The castle is home to many great paintings and has an impressive collection of English and French eighteenth-century furniture. It also houses the Border Country Life Museum which displays a history of Lowland agriculture.

The Southern Upland Way, heading both east and west, can be found at the Old Tolbooth. This building, originally built in the fourteenth century, has served both as the town's jail and council chambers, and has been burned down and rebuilt a number of times. The Tolbooth is also the annual assembly point for the Common Riding Ceremony, thought to be one of the oldest of such ceremonies in the country.

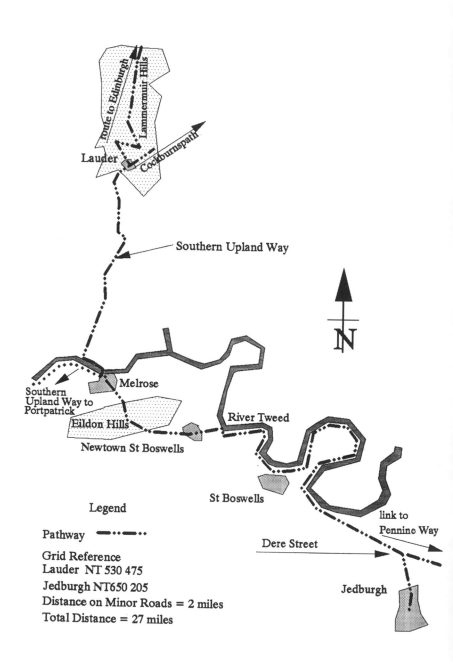

route to Edinburgh

Lammermuir Hills

Lauder

Cockburnspath

Southern Upland Way

Melrose

Southern
Upland Way to
Portpatrick

Eildon Hills

River Tweed

Newtown St Boswells

St Boswells

link to
Pennine Way

Dere Street

N

Jedburgh

Legend

Pathway —•–•—••

Grid Reference
Lauder NT 530 475
Jedburgh NT650 205
Distance on Minor Roads = 2 miles
Total Distance = 27 miles

CHAPTER NINE

Lauder to Jedburgh via the Southern Upland Way

From Lauder the first leg of this route travels to Melrose using the Southern Upland Way and is nine-and-a-half miles long. The route begins at the Tolbooth and is well signed from there. This also gives the traveller the opportunity to continue along the Southern Upland Way, taking either the remaining 32½ miles east to Cockburnspath on the North Sea coast, or heading west for 190 miles to reach Portpatrick on the coast of the Irish Sea. The official guide, written by Roger Smith and published by HMSO, describes both of these routes in detail.

For the first half mile or so the route climbs steadily up Chester Hill with the Lauder Burn in the valley below. As it continues, the route is well defined with waymarkers at regular intervals. There are also many stiles to climb as the route runs through the high pastures used by the flocks of Cheviot sheep. Here, too, there is a predominance of many types of game birds, with huge numbers of pheasants all around. As I passed through one field there seemed to be literally thousands of these birds.

After some three miles the route joins a minor road and once again commences a steady climb up Kedslie Hill. This road is thought to have been built on the line of Dere Street. The most likely route, however, would have been the lower route, still

Footbridge over Tweed at Melrose

a minor road, through Kedslie and New Brainslie and thus on to Lauder.

As it continues its journey south, this small road deteriorates in quality until it almost peters out altogether, reverting to a path as it climbs to Easter Housebyres. At this point there is a spectacular view over the Tweed Valley with Galashiels to the west, Melrose to the east and the Eildon Hills providing a splendid backdrop to this majestic scene.

From here the route descends quickly down to the banks of the Tweed at Gattonside from where it continues along the north bank until it reaches a suspension bridge. This chain-suspension bridge was designed and built by J. S. Brown in

Notice on the footbridge across the Tweed at Melrose

1826. Before crossing it, have a look up at the sign on its tower to check you are not in contravention of one of the bylaws listed – if you are, you will certainly be fined £2 or have to serve what could end up being a substantial period in one of Her Majesty's Prisons!

After crossing this bridge we bid farewell to the Southern Upland Way as it meanders along the southern bank of the Tweed west, towards Galashiels.

Turn left along the road to join Annay Road (B6360). There turn right and follow this road for a short distance into the beautiful town of Melrose. Alternatively, turn right at the suspension bridge and walk along the path for a short distance to the bowling green. Turn left along the footpath,

Melrose Abbey

crossing St Mary's Road and then continuing along the side of the Greenyards, the home of Melrose Rugby Union Football Club, one of the giants of Scottish Premier League Rugby.

Melrose's history can be traced back to the time when this area was occupied by a tribe of Ancient Britons known as the Selgovae. When the Romans arrived in the first century AD and established a fort at Trimontium, overlooked by the Eildon Hills, the Selgovae chose to trade rather than fight. But after the Roman influence finally waned this tribe was driven from the area by the Angles from Northumberland.

In the seventh century St Aiden formed a church at Mailros – a later head of this religious community was St Boisil from whom the neighbouring village of St Boswells takes its name. It was also the birthplace of Cuthbert who set up the religious community at Lindesfarn and who was ultimately canonised for his work in converting the pagan inhabitants of East Fife.

Melrose Abbey, founded by David I in 1136, was the first to be built in Scotland for the Cistercian order and was colonised by monks from Yorkshire. It was immortalised by Sir Walter Scott in the *Lay of the Last Minstrel*.

Throughout history, as with the other three Border abbeys, Melrose took the brunt of many assaults from the English. It was first destroyed by Edward II in 1322 and again by Richard II in 1385. It was finally demolished during the Rough Wooing – a phrase coined by Sir Walter Scott to describe the English invasions between 1544 and 1545. Under the leadership of the Earl of Hertford, these invasions were in revenge for Scotland breaking off the betrothal of the young Queen Mary to Prince Edward (later King Edward VI), Henry VIII's son. By this action, in which all four Border abbeys, together with Holyrood and Balerno, were sacked and put to the torch, Henry thought to force the marriage.

King Robert the Bruce's heart is buried in Melrose Abbey under the eastern window. Bruce had wanted his heart buried in the Church of the Holy Sepulchre in Jerusalem and after his death his body was interred in Dunfermline Abbey and Sir James Douglas was charged to convey the king's heart to

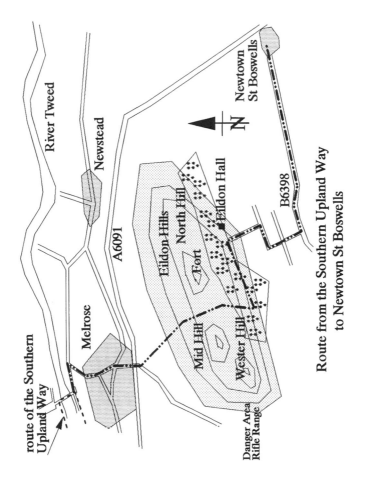

route of the Southern
Upland Way

River Tweed

Newstead

Melrose

A6091

Eildon Hills
North Hill

Fort

Eildon Hall

Mid Hill

Wester Hill

Danger Area
Rifle Range

N

Newtown
St Boswells

B6398

Route from the Southern Upland Way
to Newtown St Boswells

the Holy Land. However, while in Spain doing battle with the Moors, Douglas was himself killed and Bruce's heart was returned to Scotland and buried at Melrose.

There are many other places of interest in Melrose, such as the Motor Museum with its fine collection of vintage cars, and the walled Garden of Priorwood which is located next to the Abbey.

Carry on through Melrose via Abbey Street and Market Cross, into Lilliesleaf then go under the bridge which carries the main Galashiels Road overhead. The recently built road follows the line of the solum of the former Waverley to Berwick Railway Line and indeed Melrose Station can still be found on the footpath which runs alongside this road.

This is one of the oldest surviving railway stations in Scotland. It was built in 1849 in the Jacobean style. It was successfully saved from demolition by a petition signed by 4,000 local people and was restored to its former glory in 1985. It seems such a pity that it could not have continued to serve the local community in its original function.

Not much more than a mile along this footpath towards Galashiels is Sir Walter Scott's house, Abbotsford.

After passing under the Galashiels Road, continue into Dingleton Road where the footpath to the Eildon Hills commences about 100m on the left between two houses, at which point it is signposted. Climb up a set of steps and over a stile, keeping to the path between the two fences. Climb over two more stiles and take the route adjacent to the left-hand fence. Cross over another fence into open country and head for the saddle between the north and mid hills along the rough and sometimes very wet path.

When you reach the top of the saddle continue down the other side. Carry on past a larger track, which runs at right angles, until another such track is reached. Turn left at this junction and follow this track for about a quarter of a mile to where another junction is reached. Carry straight on here for another quarter of a mile. The track now meets a minor road. Turn right on to this road and carry on past Greenwells to

Wallace's Statue

another junction and turn right. Follow this road as it veers almost 90 degrees to reach a T-junction and again turn right. Then quickly turn left.

Carry on down this road to another T-junction and here turn left. This is the B6398. Follow this for just under a mile into Newtown St Boswells.

But before you commence all these manoeuvres, tarry a while on the Eildon Hills. Perhaps you will have to tarry longer than a while for, if you visit the site of the Eildon Tree which is marked by the Eildon Tree stone (for the tree has long-since perished), the same fate may befall you as happened to Thomas the Rymer. It was here that, tradition reports, he met a Fairy Queen and went off with her to Elfland, returning to the Eildon Tree seven years later. Indeed, it is said that Thomas actually did disappear from his home at Earlstone for seven years. It is also said that if you walk over the hills on a moonlight night you will hear the ringing of elfin bells.

Other stories of this place claim that the ancient wizard, Michael Scott, smote the hill into its triple crown and that it was the site of the Battle of Arthuret which was said to have lasted for 46 days, claiming the lives of 80,000 men. Arthur and 150 of his knights are said to sleep in caverns within the hills, still in full armour, swords and shields at the ready, waiting to rise up once again to their nation's aid.

More tangible is the site of the Roman base of Trimontium which lies at the foot of the Eildon hills. This important base was in existence for over 300 years and although no trace of it now exists there is a memorial marking its existence at the roadside near the village of Newstead.

On the north hill there is the remains of an Iron Age fort which was also the site of a Roman signal station.

On entering Newtown St Boswells the traveller will pass the headquarters of Border Council. It was decided to make this little village the capital of Borders Region to avoid causing strife amongst the many towns of great historical significance which could have quite legitimately taken on the role.

On reaching the Main Street in Newtown St Boswells, turn

Dryburgh Abbey

right and head down the hill towards the village shops. Turn left into Tweedside Road then turn left again at a signpost indicating the 'Footpath to the Glen'. The road winds down past the livestock auction market and on under the A68 past the sewage works. Here, at a small footbridge over a burn, you will find the first yellow waymarker for the Tweed Walkway.

Follow these markers along the beautiful banks of the River Tweed for five miles to Maxton, passing on the way the village of St Boswells. As this path is clearly marked it is not necessary to give many details of the route. It only remains to describe the many features of interest which the traveller will encounter along the route.

After walking for not much more than a mile along this pleasant wooded escarpment, with the beautiful River Tweed flowing below the pathway, a flight of steps descends to Dryburgh Footbridge. Our route continues along the southern bank of the river, still clearly marked by waymarkers. However, the traveller is advised to take the time to cross this bridge and explore Dryburgh Abbey and Wallace's statue which are found at Dryburgh.

After crossing the bridge, turn right and join a small road which leads to a T-junction. From here turn left for Wallace's statue and right for Dryburgh Abbey – the latter, by this time, being clearly visible at the bottom of the road.

To get to Wallace's statue walk through the tiny hamlet of Dryburgh and on up the hill for 200m or so where you will find a path to the left which is signed 'Public Footpath to Wallace's Monument'. This path winds up a wooded hill for almost a kilometre and then, suddenly, around a bend, Wallace's statue appears as a giant, only yards away at the top of the hill. As I approached this statue I felt a sense of fear, it was more than being awe inspired, I felt I had to keep repeating to myself that this man is on my side! I am a Scot, after all! He is truly an intimidating sight.

The 22-ft-high statue was commissioned by David Erskine, the eleventh Earl of Buchan and carved from a single red-

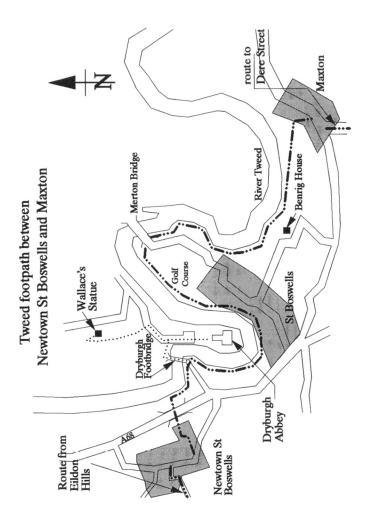

Tweed footpath between
Newtown St Boswells and Maxton

N

route to
Dere Street

Maxton

River Tweed

Merton Bridge

Benrig House

Wallace's
Statue

Golf
Course

St Boswells

Dryburgh
Footbridge

Dryburgh
Abbey

Route from
Eildon
Hills

A68

Newtown St
Boswells

sandstone block by John Smith. It was unveiled in 1814. (See chapter six.)

From the top of the hill of Wallace's statue there is a beautiful view over the River Tweed to the Eildon Hills beyond.

Retrace your steps back to Dryburgh. The original town was sacked along with the abbey by Sir George Bowes and Sir Brian Layton and 700 Englishmen in 1544, but these and other abominations were revenged the next year at the Battle of Ancrum. Neither the town nor the abbey were ever rebuilt.

Dryburgh Abbey was founded by Hugh de Morville, King David I's Norman constable, between 1140 and 1150. As with Melrose, Kelso and Jedburgh it took the brunt of many assaults from the English, being destroyed by Edward II in 1322 and again by Richard II in 1385.

After the Reformation in 1560 the abbey and its lands passed into the hands of the Erskine family.

The ruins of the abbey lie in beautiful and tranquil surroundings, abounded by elm, cedar, sycamore, and oak a peaceful and fitting burial place for Sir Walter Scott whose grave is in the North Choir Chapel.

Retrace your steps back across Dryburgh Footbridge to recommence the journey along the Tweed and within a short distance you will reach the village of St Boswells.

St Boswells takes its name from St Boisil, although there is no record of any settlement during the time that this saint lived at the monastery of Auld Mailros a mile or so to the north. The village hosts Boisil's Fair every July and has done so since before the seventeenth century. The fair was once a most important horse-trading event attracting traders, dealers and farmers from the length and breadth of the country.

The path carries alongside St Boswells golf course to Mertoun Bridge. Here you can see many varieties of waterfowl and wild duck.

Shortly after passing Mertoun Bridge, the walkway splits into two paths. Carry on over a bridge and continue along the riverside. The other path, which veers to the right and cuts inland, heads up to the east side of St Boswells.

A little further on the path once again splits in two. This time take the path to the right as it climbs up a set of steps adjacent to a wall. This is known locally as Jacob's Ladder. The path passes a well, set into the wall which encloses Benrig House, which is called the Well's St Boisils.

At the top of these steps turn left and follow this high path alongside a graveyard before it descends once more to lower ground and crosses over a track. After crossing the track, continue along the path through a small wood. Then go up another set of steps to where the path comes out at Maxton Church. Just outside the churchyard is the only relic left of the railway in this area – a station platform seat with Maxton emblazoned upon it.

The path soon joins the A699 road which goes through the village of Maxton. Turn right and walk along this road for 100m or so to the next junction which is signed for Longnewton. Carry along this road until you come to a road on the left signed Morridgehall. Follow this road as it turns through 90 degrees, passes a farmyard and reverts to a track.

Carry on along this track to a gate on the other side of which is a footpath. To the left of this footpath is the first waymarker with the little Roman helmet which represents Dere Street. This path is only about 100m in length.

Dere Street, the road constructed by the Romans from Tees to Forth is sometimes incorrectly referred to as Watling Street. The latter is further south. The name Dere Street was given to the road by the Saxons. The road was constructed by order of the Emperor Agricola to link Roman Britain on the south of Hadrian's Wall with the fortifications on Inveresk Hill on the River Forth at Musselburgh and at Caer Almond at Cramond.

After 100m the path as such disappears and the way follows a line through a series of fields crossed by many stiles. The way is easy enough to follow thanks to the waymarkers. These fields, calm and tranquil as they are today, were once the killing fields, for this is the site of the Battle of Ancrum Moor fought in 1545 as part of the Rough Wooing by Henry VIII. The English under Sir Ralph Eure were brutally defeated by

Resting place of Sir Walter Scott in Dryburgh Abbey

Jedburgh Abbey

the Red Douglas, Earl of Angus, for defacing the tombs of the Douglases, who had fallen at Otterburn almost two centuries earlier, at Melrose Abbey.

It was at this battle that the fair maiden, Lilliard of Maxton, on seeing her lover cut down in battle, joined the fray and fought with much ferocity until she herself was killed. The inscription on her nearby tomb reads:

> Fair Maiden Lilliard, under this stane
> Little was her stature, but muckle was her fame.
> Upon English loons she laid mony thomps,
> And when her legs were cuttit off, she faught upon her
> stumps.

More than two hundred years later, a farmer who was ploughing a field hereabouts turned up a sword reckoned to be from this battle, which was ultimately presented to Sir Walter Scott.

The way then goes through a ridge of trees before coming out once more on to open countryside where a narrow, but well-defined, path commences. After about three miles the path crosses a minor road and then cuts through Divet Ha Wood and crosses the B6400. On the other side of this road, clearly signposted, is Harestanes Woodland Centre. The visitors' centre at Harestanes has been adapted from the original sawmill of the Monteviot Estate and houses a natural history exhibition. There is also a tea-room where the hungry traveller can find refreshment.

This estate was owned by the Kerr family who form the line of the Marquess of Lothian. Monteviot House is still owned by the family but most of the estate has been handed over to Borders Council who run Harestanes Woodland Centre in conjunction with Lothian Estates.

There are many interesting walks at Harestanes, including one to Peniel Heugh which means High Hill. On top of this hill stands a large monument which was commissioned by the sixth Marquess of Lothian to commemorate the Duke of Wellington and the Battle of Waterloo. The monument, which was started in 1815, was not finished until 1826, a year after the death of the Marquess. It stands on the site of an Iron Age fort, the earthworks of which are still visible.

Within the woodland centre are some unusual trees, such as Lawson cypress, Norway spruce, Wellingtonia (a type of North American redwood), monkey puzzle and box trees.

Whether you are on the path to the Woodland Centre or coming from the visitors' centre, follow the blue route which will eventually take you out at Monteviot Suspension Bridge. Dere Street continues on the other side.

After crossing the bridge, turn left and follow the River Teviot.

After a mile or so the path leaves the banks of the River Teviot and joins those of the Jed Water. After a short distance of about 300m the path joins the A68. Walk north across the bridge and on the other side of the road the route is once again signposted along a minor road.

This is the first of three places by which the traveller can leave Dere Street and head for Jedburgh. Simply follow this minor road which runs parallel to both the A68 and Jed Water for a further two miles into Jedburgh.

After about 100m the route of Dere Street strikes east using another minor road which, very quickly, reverts to a track. The route climbs steeply up to high ground, offering good views along the length of the Jed Valley.

At the top of this hill is the second exit point from Dere Street into Jedburgh. Take a small path to the right. It is the first path located on this part of the route, but take care as it may be easily missed. This small path winds downhill again, joining a minor road at a farm called Mount Ullston. From here it joins up with the first minor road, described above, about quarter of a mile from Jedburgh.

However, if you ignore both of these exits and carry along the route of Dere Street for another three-quarters of a mile, you will come to a crossroads where you'll find the third route to Jedburgh. Just turn right and follow this minor road for a mile and a half into this beautiful and historic Border town.

If you are tempted to carry further along Dere Street, remember that Jedburgh is the last point of civilisation before crossing into England. Even after the Border is crossed, there are still a few more miles to negotiate before arriving at the village of Byrness. The distance between Jedburgh and Byrness is 20 miles, climbing to a height of over 500m at Brown Heart Law and again at Hungry Law.

This ancient burgh of Jedburgh is situated in the sheltered valley of the Jed Water. Here, too, stretching over many miles, was once the site of Jed Forest, the famous hunting ground of Scottish kings.

There is evidence that a settlement at Jedburgh has existed for as long as 3,000 years. The name, which seems originally to have been Jedworth, simply means the hamlet on the River Jed. During the Roman occupation, this valley would almost certainly have contained a sizable garrison.

The town today is a busy market town containing many buildings of great historical significance.

Jedburgh Castle has existed on this site since the twelfth century. It was handed over to England as part of the Treaty of Falaise in 1174 when William the Lion, then a prisoner of the English King Henry II, was forced to give up his title of Earl of Huntington and surrender the castles of Roxburgh, Jedburgh, Berwick, Edinburgh, and Stirling. Malcolm IV died in the castle in 1165 and it was finally demolished in 1409 to keep it from English hands. It has since lain in ruins.

The castle which exists today was built on the site of the original and is, in fact, Castle Gaol which was built in 1823. It has not served this purpose for some time, and it now houses the Museum of Social History.

Jedburgh Abbey was founded by David I as a priory in 1138. Twenty years later, when the town was granted the status of a royal burgh, it was made an abbey. Jedburgh and its abbey were burned by the English several times, but although the abbey was destroyed in 1545, after the Reformation it continued as the parish kirk until 1875.

Parts of this ruin are almost intact. The twelfth-century

Autumn in Dere Street

Romanesque doorway, at the west end of the building, has more or less survived unscathed. So, too, have the internal columns which separate the nave from the aisles.

The town's Mercat Cross is dominated on its south side by Newgate steeple, which once housed the town prison. This prison, with its condemned cell, is open to the public.

The remains of the Franciscan Friary, built around the

beginning of the sixteenth century and also destroyed by the English in 1545, was excavated in 1983. Now only its foundations are visible.

The house known as Mary Queen of Scots's house and which was owned by the Kerrs of Ferniehurst, one of the important families of the district, was used by the Queen whilst presiding over the court of justice. She became gravely ill in this house after making a 40-mile trip to visit the Earl of Bothwell who had been wounded in a border skirmish. She later married Bothwell, a factor which contributed greatly to her ultimate downfall.

Charles Edward Stuart (Bonnie Prince Charlie) lodged in a house in Castlegate in 1745 before his attempt to invade England.

The national bard, Robert Burns, also lodged in the town in 1787 whilst on a tour of the Borders. According to Burns, he was presented with the freedom of the town at this time. However, no official record of this ceremony exists.

William and Dorothy Wordsworth spent a holiday in Jedburgh in 1803, staying in a house in Abbey Close. During this time the couple were visited by Walter Scott who read them the yet unpublished *Lay of the Last Minstrel*.

Within High Street, which is the main street of the town, is the location of the Spread-Eagle Hotel which is the oldest continually inhabited inn in Scotland and thought to also have been visited by Mary Queen of Scots.

Continue your journey along the length of this street and on to Castle Hill where the game of Hand Ba' is played every February.

The game is said to originate from a Scottish victory over the English when the victors used the heads of their enemies as the balls. It is played between the Uppies and the Doonies – the teams being picked according to whether their residence is above or below Mercat Cross.

These are only a few of the interesting places and events in Jedburgh. Enough, I hope, to whet the appetite and encourage you to spend some time visiting this beautiful town.

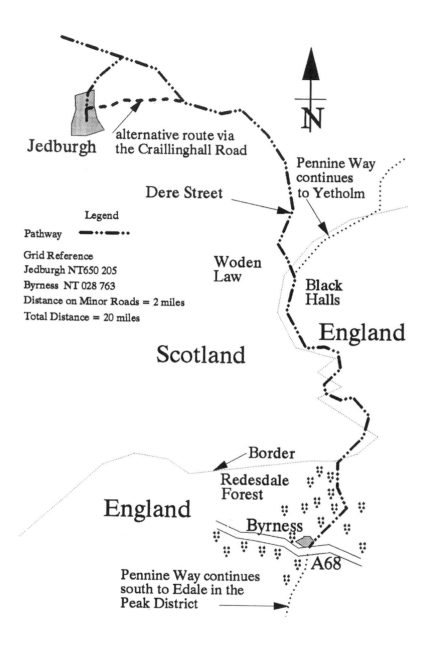

Jedburgh

alternative route via
the Craillinghall Road

Pennine Way
continues
to Yetholm

Dere Street

Legend

Pathway

Grid Reference
Jedburgh NT650 205
Byrness NT 028 763
Distance on Minor Roads = 2 miles
Total Distance = 20 miles

Woden
Law

Black
Halls

England

Scotland

Border

Redesdale
Forest

England

Byrness

A68

Pennine Way continues
south to Edale in the
Peak District

N

CHAPTER TEN

The Link with the Pennine Way

For this final leg of the Central Scottish Way, we leave Jedburgh and continue along Dere Street until reaching the Pennine Way. Return to the crossroads where the trip along Dere Street was terminated.

A word of warning first! The terrain that you will experience on your journey southwards, although not particularly difficult underfoot, should be viewed as a serious and strenuous hill walk and the proper equipment should be used. Suitable clothing and footwear must be worn and the relevant ordnance survey maps and a compass should also be carried. Without meaning to insult my readers, I have to say that the ability to use a map and compass is, of course, a necessity!

I must also at this point reiterate the information which I gave at the end of the last chapter. The distance between Jedburgh and Byrness is 20 miles climbing to a height of over 500m at Brown Heart Law and again at Hungry Law. Expect to spend a whole day or more travelling this part of the journey.

Dere Street is well signed as far as Tow Ford, before which the remains of the Roman camp at Pennymuir are located on the right of the minor road which forms part of the Roman road at this point. This is the best preserved of the Roman temporary camps in Scotland. When occupied the camp would

The author takes a rest at the end of the Pennine Way

have enclosed a rectangular area of about 40 acres, around which would have been the typical earthen ramparts.

The north and west ramparts are still visible today, standing some 4½ feet high alongside a 12ft-wide external ditch. The outline of the camp can be clearly seen from Woden Law.

After leaving Tow Ford, it is relatively easy to follow Dere Street. However, because it is not signed, I recommend that you consult Ordnance Survey Sheet 80. The street climbs steadily up to the shoulder of Woden Law from where it is not much of a diversion to reach the summit. Here are the remains of an Iron Age hill-fort which consist of a stone wall and two outer ramparts with a ditch between. This hill-fort was constructed by the Selgovae and was taken over by the Romans as a practice-ground for siege training.

Once back on Dere Street the route continues between Hunthall Hill and Blackhall Hill and then past Garsty Law to where the Pennine Way joins Dere Street at Black Halls and the border between Scotland and England.

From here the route continues south to the extensive Roman camp at Chew Green within Northumberland. After passing this camp, Dere Street and the Pennine Way part company.

Our journey briefly follows the Pennine Way to return back over the Border into Scotland before once again crossing into England at Ogre Hill.

Follow the Pennine Way as it skirts the north-eastern part of the Redesdale Forest which is within Northumberland National Park. Then go past Houx Hill and Byrness Hill. Finally, the straight path descends quickly down to the small village of Byrness.

This village was created at the turn of the century to house the workers and their families who were brought to the area to construct the nearby Catcleugh Reservoir which took 15 years to complete. Later these workers were used to plant the Border Forest.

Once at Byrness, you have the option of walking the further 230 miles to the end of the Pennine Way at Edale in the Peak District.

By the time you reach Byrness, you will have travelled from the flat central belt of Scotland to the hills of Lammermuirs, Eildons and Cheviots and through the beautiful valleys of the Scottish Border Country.

I feel sure the memory of this route will be recalled with lasting fondness by you as it is by me.

BIBLIOGRAPHY

Border Country, by Edmond Bogg (John Samson) York, 1898

Borrowstounness and District, by T.J. Salmon (Hodge & Co) 1913

A Dictionary of Scottish History, by Gordon Donaldson and Robert S. Morpeth (John Donald) Edinburgh

Dictionary of Scottish Place Names, by Mike Darton (Lochar Publishing)

The Edinburgh and Glasgow Union Canal, by Alison Massey (Falkirk Museums)

Historic Musselburgh, by James Wilkie

Historic South Edinburgh, by Charles J. Smith and Charles Skilton in *The Scots Magazine* (Scotsman Publications)

The History and Antiquities of Roxburghshire, Vols 1, 2 and 3, by Alexander Jeffrey (Walter Easton), Jedburgh, 1855

History of Cumbernauld and Kilsyth, by Hugo Millar (Cumbernauld Historical Society)

In the Lap of the Lammermuirs, by William McConachie (William Blackwood & Sons) Edinburgh, 1913

The Intelligent Traveller's Guide to Historic Scotland, by Philip A. Crowl (Sidgwick & Jackson) London

Kilsyth History Trail, by J. Gordon (Kilsyth Civic Trust)

The Second City, by C.A. Oakley (Blackie)